OLD LAW—NEW LIFE

D0974455

OLD LAW—NEW LIFE

*The Ten Commandments
and
New Testament Faith*

Earl F. Palmer

ABINGDON PRESS
NASHVILLE

OLD LAW—NEW LIFE

Copyright © 1984 by Abingdon Press

All rights reserved.
No part of this book may be reproduced in any manner
whatsoever without written permission of the publisher
except brief quotations embodied in critical articles or
reviews. For information address Abingdon Press,
Nashville, Tennessee.

Library of Congress Cataloging in Publication Data

PALMER, EARL F.
  Old law—new life.
  Bibliography: p.
  1. Ten commandments. 2. Law and gospel. 3. Law
(Theology) I. Title
BV4655.P329 1984   222′1606   84-3103

ISBN 0-687-28744-8

Scripture quotations in this publication unless other-
wise noted are from the Revised Standard Version of the
Bible, copyrighted 1946, 1952, © 1971, 1973.

MANUFACTURED BY THE PARTHENON PRESS AT
NASHVILLE, TENNESSEE, UNITED STATES OF AMERICA

To
Robert Boyd Munger
teacher and friend

Contents

Preface

These are my ultimate attitudes towards life; the soils for the seeds of doctrine. These in some dark way I thought before I could write, and felt before I could think: that we may proceed more easily afterwards, I will roughly recapitulate them now. I felt in my bones; first, that this world does not explain itself. It may be a miracle with a supernatural explanation; it may be a conjuring trick, with a natural explanation. But the explanation of the conjuring trick, if it is to satisfy me, will have to be better than the natural explanations I have heard. The thing is magic, true or false. Second, I came to feel as if magic must have a meaning and meaning must have someone to mean it. There was something personal in the world, as in a work of art; whatever it meant it meant violently. Third, I thought this purpose beautiful in its old design, in spite of its defects, such as dragons. Fourth, that the proper form of thanks to it is some form of humility and restraint; we should thank God for beer and Burgundy by not drinking too much of them. We owed, also, an obedience to whatever made us. And last, and strangest, there had come into my mind a vague and vast impression that in some way all good was a remnant to be stored and held sacred out of some primordial ruin. Man had saved his good as Crusoe saved his goods: he had saved them from a wreck. All this I felt and the age gave me no encouragement to feel it. And all this time I had not even thought of Christian theology. (G. K. Chesterton, *Orthodoxy*)

The five intuitions that G. K. Chesterton felt at a very deep level were an essential part of his life before anyone told him of the significance of the law and the gospel, the law of Moses or the gospel of Jesus Christ. What the young Chesterton felt was something of an inner consensus, an agreement that had been drawn together out of the experiences of his life. They are like the pathways of a dozen different wanderings that were beginning to converge into his mind and soul as that which he counted upon to be true and necessary.

He depended upon these five sources, and he was building his life upon them, all of which made this young man restless and inquisitive. Eventually, he discovered for himself the fulfillment of his intuitions and the quest that went with them when he met the God of the Bible. His expectations were both surprised and fulfilled by the one whom he was to call the "Enormous Exception"—the one who is the Lord of the law and the Lord of the gospel.

This book of mine is about the event in human history where the grand consensus, the new agreement, was first made known to the human family. It happened to a real people in a real place. They were refugees on their journey through the deserts of Sinai, the date was 1290 B.C., and the event was the Ten Commandments. Nothing would ever be the same again for that people of Mount Sinai, and within a short time what they experienced would become a universal gift for the people of all the earth.

The Ten Commandments are more than ten commandments! They are the concrete, understandable breakthrough of the character, the promise, and the will of God into the roadways and cross streets of our daily lives. There is a mystery about this holy agreement because it gathers into itself the yearnings and intuitions of the human story; it also points beyond itself toward its author. This strong law is more than legal code; it is a map; it is the grand design, the lyrical poem, and most of all the first speech by the God who is able to speak for himself.

My commentary is a theological inquiry into the meaning of the Ten Commandments. Though I have endeavored at each step of the way to discuss the technical issues that are relevant to the discussion, my first concern has been to explore the theological significance of the law of Moses within its Old Testament and New Testament settings. From that standpoint, I have tried to ask the discipleship questions so that our study will dare to relate the theological questions to our own contemporary lives. My perspective is that of a Christian who recognizes the law as that which reveals the will of God.

I am indebted to many people who have been my teachers and my companions in the challenge of this study. I want to express special thanks to my colleagues in ministry and the people at First Presbyterian Church in Berkeley where I serve as pastor. I appreciate my school, Princeton Theological Seminary, and especially Jack Cooper, Ron White and the staff at Adams House where I have done most of the research for this book. Most of all, I want to say thank you to my family for their enthusiasm, encouragement, and love—Shirley and our children, Anne, Jon, and Elizabeth.

Earl F. Palmer
Berkeley, California

Introduction

For Christians of the twentieth century, what is the importance of the ancient law first given to Moses at Mount Sinai? Do we really need the law of Moses now that history has passed it by and we have more current standards for judgment under God for courtroom and place of worship? Has not the law, the Ten Commandments, been fulfilled in Jesus Christ?

It will take time to develop adequate answers to these questions, but let me try to answer the basic question first.

The Ten Commandments are of great importance for two reasons, both of which are vitally significant to New Testament Christianity. First, the Ten Commandments present the heart of the Old Testament, the consensus of Israel's life and thought, and it is impossible to understand the New

Testament gospel apart from this Old Testament gospel. The experience of a real people in a real place is the ground from which this Christian good news emerges as God's fulfillment of that which he began much earlier. It is simply a fact that we cannot make sense of the first-century fulfillment journey separated from the earlier part of that journey.

In his book on the Old Testament, *The Creative Word*, Walter Brueggemann notes this initial role of the law in Israel's life. "Regarding the Torah, I shall argue that it is a statement of community ethos, a definitional statement of the character of the community which is a given and is not negotiable among the new generation" (p. 10). If this were the only reason to study carefully the law of Moses, it would be an important reason. The twentieth-century Christian cannot experience a healthy faith without a living connection to the root system from which that faith has come. In the same way that children at all periods of their life need relationship with parents in order to really understand their own contemporary identity, so Christian faith cannot stay healthy apart from the communion of saints and the rich history that accompanies the journey from Abraham the father, through Moses the deliverer, to David the king, to Jesus of Nazareth, the Lord and Savior. It is a long history, and each part of that story is connected both to that which comes before and to that which comes after. The nonnegotiable consensus covenant that held the community of the journey together is the Torah, and therefore we must always understand its intent and its influence in the life of Israel.

But there is an even more fundamental importance to the law for us today. The Ten Commandments express the will of God for life. They teach God's will for human life, and in that instruction they give to us a primary understanding of the meaning of our own humanity. This fundamental importance of the law has not been dismissed or overruled by the teaching of the New Testament. Though the New Testament writers follow their Lord in opposing legalism and the trivialization of the law, the New Testament in no way reduces the theological vitality or crucial significance of the law of Mount Sinai for the life of God's people, both for Jews and Greeks. "It is evident that Jesus regarded the Ten Commandments as the revealed will of God. . . . Jesus moved in a direction strongly opposed by Rabbinic Judaism. The law was not to be viewed as a series of stipulations all on the same level. Rather, behind all the laws lay the one will of God" (Brevard Childs, *The Book of Exodus: A Critical, Theological Commentary*, p. 429).

It will be our intent to examine closely the law that Moses received following the Exodus from Egypt. We shall consider the text of the Ten Commandments as they appear in Exodus 20 and Deuteronomy 5 as a whole fabric document, since that is the way the law makes its appearance in the Bible and was understood in the life and times of Israel. The history of Old Testament research has assigned these two texts to various times and sources for authorship and collection. The most recent linguistic research makes the arguments for late authorship, as S. R. Driver's in *Deuteronomy* in the International Critical Commentary (1895), without foundation. Driver calls for authorship of the Ten Commandments at the time of the middle prophets, but his linguistic arguments are discredited by the recent demonstration of the very early development of the Hebrew language. I see no convincing reasons for contradicting the tradition of the Old Testament, which assigned these texts to the earliest strands of Old Testament literature. Moses is the most likely source of these documents just as the tradition of Israel has stubbornly maintained.

1

Torah

When the Old Testament describes the covenant and the commandments that the people of Israel received at Mount Sinai, the word that is used is *torah*.

The root system of the word *torah* is as interesting as the word itself. Its basic root is the Hebrew word *yāra*, which means in its most literal sense "to throw," "to cast." The idea is to throw out a stone. Therefore this primitive concrete meaning develops into the idea of "to lead, to guide, to point out the way." The word *yāra* is used in Genesis 46:28, when Jacob sends forth his son Judah on a mission: "He sent Judah before him to Joseph to *show the way* before him in Goshen."

When the consonant "m" is attached to this root word *yāra*, the word becomes *moreh*, which is a word for "teacher." This is the word in Proverbs 5:13, "I did not listen to the voice of my *teachers*."

When the consonant "t" is attached to *yāra*, the word becomes *torah*. This word appears in the Old Testament 221 times, and becomes one of its three or four most important words. It is usually translated by the English word "law," as in Deuteronomy 4:44. "This is the *law* which Moses set before the children of Israel." Notice in this sentence how dynamic a word *torah* is within the sentence—it is not so much a "code" as it is a "way."

Other English word choices are sometimes used by translators for the word *torah*, as in Isaiah 30:9, "who will not hear the *instruction* of the LORD."

It is clear from the root sense of *torah* and also by the way this word is used throughout the Old Testament that *torah* has within it the strong and dynamic sense of "the way," "the right way." One Jewish scholar, Andre Neher, makes this observation: "The Hebrew word *torah* does not signify order but orientation. It is not a law, it is the way, the road along which a common enterprise is possible" (Neher, *Moses and the Vocation of the Jewish People*). We feel this quality intensely when we read the beautiful law psalm (Ps. 1), because of the contrast present: "Blessed is the man who walks not in the counsel of the wicked . . . but his delight is in the law of the LORD. . . . for the LORD knows the way of the righteous, but the way of the wicked will perish." Notice also Psalm 119: "Blessed are those whose way is blameless, who walk in the law of the LORD" (v. 1).

Torah is therefore a word that describes the roadway; it is basic and down to earth; it is a word that expresses God's will for the way we are to journey in our lives. A teacher, a *moreh*, points toward the way accurately, so that the teacher's pupil is able to find the place where the way leads. The *moreh* throws the rock clearly and straight ahead; so in a similar fashion the law shows the way.

The Torah is, in the Old Testament, the revelation to us by God of the true way. It is like a pointer or a map, a faithful signpost that shows the right path. In view of the meaning of *torah*, it is instructive to note that the Hebrew word translated "blessed," *asher*, which is the word used in Psalms 1 and 119, means in its literal sense "to find the way." Therefore Psalm 119:1 could be translated, "You have found the *right way* when your path is blameless and when you walk in the *Torah* of the Lord." That is to say—the blessed person is the person who has found the will of God and who follows the pathway of that holy will.

See how movement-oriented and how dynamic is the Old Testament portrayal of the law! The law of Moses should not therefore become a static document that a community or court of law refers to in certain extreme or technical instances. Rather, by original design it is intended to be the daily guide for the daily life of the people. We can now better understand what Brueggemann means by his description of the Torah as the "ethos" of the people.

The Jews were not the first people to have a tradition of law. Researchers have now been able to translate and understand other examples of ancient law that predate the time of Moses and the Exodus. The codes of Eshruna and of Hammurabi are two examples. The most famous is the Code of

Hammurabi, which has been given the ancient date of 1750 B.C.

There are interesting similarities between the Code of Hammurabi and the case laws given in Exodus, Leviticus, and Deuteronomy. But there is a sharp contrast between the Code of Hammurabi and the Ten Commandments. The Ten Commandments are *apodictic* law, whereas the Code of Hammurabi is *casuistic* law. What we mean by that description is that the Code of Hammurabi is case law, written in the style of "when . . . , if . . . ," whereas the Ten Commandments are stated in "short, positive, declaratory sentences" (see Jack Finegan, *Let My People Go*, discussion pp. 123-27).

Here is a sample from the Code of Hammurabi #251: "If a man's bull have been wont to gore and they have made known to him his habit of goring, and he have not protected his horns or have not tied him up, and that bull gore the son of a man and bring about his death, he shall pay one-half mina of silver." We find almost the identical law in Exodus: "But if the ox has been accustomed to gore in the past, and its owner has been warned but has not kept it in, and it kills a man or a woman, the ox shall be stoned, and its owner also shall be put to death. If a ransom is laid on him, then he shall give for the redemption of his life whatever is laid upon him" (Exod. 21:29-30). This is case law.

When we come to the law of Mount Sinai, however, we find something totally different. Something new is happening, and it has to do not only with the way to live, the roadway, but also with the Lord of the roadway. At Mount Sinai a relationship is being announced that goes far beyond anything known or expressed in case law. The psalmist who wrote the hymn in Psalm 81 understood the dramatic difference. Listen to the psalm.

Hear, O my People, while I admonish you!
O Israel, if you would but listen to me!
There shall be no strange gods among you;
You shall not bow down to a foreign god.
I am the LORD your God, who brought you up out of the land of Egypt.
Open your mouth wide and I will fill it.
. . . .
O that my people would listen to me,
That Israel would walk in my ways! (Ps. 81:8-10, 13)

This is law at a deeper level than mere regulation or requirements concerning technical situations.

The Ten Commandments are unique in the ancient world. Because of that uniqueness, Israel would become a people deeply imprinted by this special mark of the law of Mount Sinai. Even though they were unsuccessful in obeying the law of God, nevertheless they knew that they were under it; it was permanently imprinted into their character. In an odd sense Israel was both better off because of the Ten Commandments and at the same time in more distress because of the Ten Commandments. That fact had not changed by the time and writing of the New Testament. Torah seen in its fulfillment continues to be portrayed in the language of the roadway. In his commentary on the law which we call the Sermon on the Mount (Matt. 5–7), Jesus begins with strong echoes of Psalm 1. "Blessed are the poor in spirit. . . ." The nine "blesseds" that begin that sermon recall for us the opening of Psalm 1. And, like Psalms 1 and 119, it is dominated by roadway language. "Enter by the narrow gate; . . . for the gate is narrow and the way is hard, that leads to life . . ." (Matt. 7:14).

Jesus insists upon the permanent importance of the Torah as the holy revelation of the will of God for all of time. "Think not that I have come to abolish the law and the prophets; I have come not to abolish them but to fulfil them" (Matt. 5:17).

In the Torah God has revealed his grand design for life. He has made it known to the whole human family through a refugee people in the deserts of Sinai. Like a great teacher, he has thrown the rock out ahead along the precarious path to show the way. That was the meaning of Torah. It still is!

2

Hear, O Israel

The Ten Commandments occupy a central place in the faith and theology of the Old Testament. Among biblical scholars, however, especially of the late nineteenth and early twentieth centuries, the Ten Commandments have gone through a stormy interpretive history. By the late nineteenth century, Old Testament scholars did not seriously treat the Ten Commandments as a document from the time of Moses and the Exodus. S. R. Driver, in his 1895 International Critical Commentary on Deuteronomy, places the date of the development of the Ten Commandments at the time of the prophets, some five or six hundred years later than the time of Moses and the Exodus. He has no reasons to offer for such a late date, apart from documentary theories of the formation of the Pentateuch that dominated much of nineteenth-century scholarship.

The late date he chooses is opposed to the tradition of the Jews concerning the Mount Sinai origin of the Ten Commandments.

Driver and the German school of Old Testament criticism of that time were operating upon what we now know is a faulty understanding of the development of the Hebrew language. That one misunderstanding on their part flawed all of the subsequent work in the text. We now know that the development of the Hebrew language is much more ancient than 1200 B.C. Early in our own century, Old Testament scholarship recognized this fact, which has changed the theological and critical appraisal of the texts. There is now no convincing reason to question the literacy of Moses and the Jews of his period. This development in recent Hebrew language studies has restored the ancient period of Jewish history and has made us much more respectful in our treatment of the Mosaic period.

Another scholarly battle concerning the first five Old Testament books has centered on their various sources and ingredient influences from within the history of Israel. Form criticism, which is the critical method of research that seeks to understand the historical settings of ancient documents as a clue to their interpretation, has developed various hypotheses concerning the different source influences in the Pentateuch. But the danger in this scholarly enterprise is that the basic literary approach to a document such as the Ten Commandments, and the narratives that surround it, is set aside in favor of a fascination with elaborate source theories.

For example, during the last few years, the debates about von Rad's hypothesis concerning the Exodus tradition versus the Sinai tradition have sometimes become a substitute for a serious consideration of the text as a whole as it stands in the Pentateuch. Professor Brevard Childs puts the matter very well in his observation about that particular debate: "Both approaches have failed to deal seriously with the present form of the biblical text and have focused their major interest on some phase of the prehistory . . . in fact, the history of research has often demonstrated how effectively the study of the prehistory has functioned in obscuring the biblical text through false parallels and mistaken ideas of historical development" (*Book of Exodus*, pp. 338-39).

The Ten Commandments are presented to the reader in two places in the Old Testament: Exodus 20 and Deuteronomy 5. There are some differences between the two texts which we will note within this study, but they are in essential agreement as to meaning. We will study those texts as they stand in the Hebrew Bible. What is it that we find? The Ten Commandments are by all assessments a remarkable document both in their own setting in the Old Testament and in the setting of the ancient Semitic world. In his commentary on the book of Exodus, Professor Childs notes sixteen features about the Ten Commandments that are noteworthy (pp. 377-78).

1. The Law begins with an introductory statement.
2. There is a self-introduction at the opening of

the Law in which the Lord of the Law identifies Himself.

3. The majority of the commandments are
   negative in their formal language.
4. There is no sense of metrical pattern in the
   commandments; some of the commands are
   brief and some are long.
5. The clauses that join the commandments show
   great variation in style.
6. Grammatically the commandments do not
   maintain the first person throughout.
7. The commands do consistently maintain the
   second person throughout.
8. The exact enumeration of the number 10 is not
   obvious in the text of the commandments.
9. Nowhere is there within the text a guideline as
   to how to divide the commandments into two
   tablets.
10. There is a sense of overall design in the
    commandments.
11. The casuistic style of case law is not repre-
    sented within the Ten Commandments.
12. There are parallels to the various separate laws
    of the Ten Commandments found through the
    Old Testament, but never any to the whole.
13. The are no sanctions to be found in the Ten
    Commandments, as, for example, the provi-
    sion for community penalty when the Law is
    broken—i.e., the death penalty.
14. There is no distinction made within the Ten
    Commandments between religious and ethical
    laws.

15. The commandments are marked by their stark objectivity and apparent unconcern with inner motives.
16. The Ten Commandments, except for the great introduction, has only one reference to a specific historical period and particular institution (the exodus from Egypt and the Sabbath in Deut. 5).

The law begins with the introduction and the self-disclosure of the Lawgiver himself. Both the introduction and the self-disclosure are made in a concrete historical fashion. "So Moses went down to the people and told them. And God spoke these words saying, 'I am the LORD your God, who brought you out of the land of Egypt, out of the house of bondage' " (Exod. 19:25–20:2). These are the sentences of self-disclosure.

Before Israel hears a single commandment, she is introduced to the one who speaks and is reminded of the redemption of the people out of bondage. The one who now shows Israel the way of freedom from inner tyranny is the one who had earlier set the people free from outer tyranny.

The Ten Commandments begin with the self-disclosure of the love of God. God's love is portrayed not in theoretical language but by the act which God did in history. Love in the Bible is not salvation by mimeograph, nor it is merely verbalized; rather, it is the event that happens. We find this same mixture of word and work in the whole of the Bible. When the Apostle seeks to express the love of Jesus Christ to the Corinthians, he points to an event: "I decided to know nothing among you except Jesus Christ and him crucified" (I Cor. 2:2). The love of Jesus Christ is an event that happened and happens. In the very same way the Ten Commandments begin with the assurance of an event that happened to the lives of real people in a real place. They originate from the God of redemption, who knows about the suffering of people in bondage and who knows how to set people free from bondage.

This note of hope and grace stands at the beginning of the commandments. We must never forget this origin of the Torah, or we will have distorted the law in its intention. The very helpful theological formula "law and gospel" should really be spoken as follows: "gospel and law and gospel." What I mean is that the goodness of God's redeeming love is at the source of the law as well as at the law's fulfillment.

3

Moses

The year 1290 B.C. is one of the most important dates in Israel's history. This is the most commonly accepted date for the Exodus since the archaeological excavations at Jericho. A towering figure came into the life of Israel; his name was Moses. God chose this man. He was to learn (and teach to his people) the holy name of God—*Yahweh*. He was to lead the little nation of prisoner people out of Egypt where they had become an enslaved population.

At the beginning of their Exodus experience, the people of Israel are emergency-oriented; they are held together because of common danger and a common escape goal. Once beyond the range of Egyptian troops, another challenge faces them—the challenge of how to live together on a day-to-day basis.

This same challenge faces every revolutionary movement when it finally succeeds in defeating its oppressor. What do we do after the revolution? What do we do after the escape out of the prison camps of the Nile? Joy Davidman puts the question this way: "You can't drown all the time. Sooner or later you have to start merely living again; you reach shore, sputter the water out of your lungs—and then what?" (*Smoke on the Mountain*, p. 16).

There are several options.

1. Moses can continue as the absolute leader of the people. He will hold singular power, and, though he will lend it to a small elite around him, the real power resides with him. All decisions will finally originate from him, from a human point of reference. This is the totalitarian solution to the challenge of how to live in the wilderness.

2. An opposite possibility is anarchy. The community breaks apart into factions which then proceed to create downward power formations on a smaller scale. Instead of one central source of authority, there develops a random assortment of smaller totalitarian arrangements.

Both of these solutions produce grave problems for individuals as well as society. Rule by the decree of a single leader and his chosen circle provides no protection for the ruled against the ruler. The leader such as Moses, with his special relationship with God, is beyond any effective check or balance, since there are no available criteria for judging him. The inevitable tendency in authoritarianism is toward the operating principle of "might makes right." In such a social situation, the key to survival for individual members is to establish favorable connections with those who are higher up the pyramid of power. The result is ethically and spiritually demoralizing—persons are tempted continually to sell out convictions and integrity to reap the benefits and rewards of power. The proximity to power is what matters more than anything else.

But if totalitarianism is destructive and dehumanizing to both the ruled and the rulers, anarchy is no better. With anarchy the single pyramid collapses. In its place are set up a thousand smaller but equally and really more terrifying tyrannical structures. Instead of the danger of the emperor, there is the danger of the gangster and roving bands of private armies. The Israelites experienced both of these options during their journey in the wilderness. Early in their sojournings everything depended upon the actual presence of Moses as absolute leader; when he was present, the social whole was held together by his authority. But when Moses was absent from the people, then the terror of anarchy broke out within the encampment.

The experience of Israel in the wilderness is not unique. The swings from totalitarianism to anarchy are the experience of most of the people of the human story and their societies throughout human history. Anarchy is not only a political phenomenon, it is a psychological and spiritual phenomenon as well. People lurch from the chaos of isolation and practical anarchy to the strong attachment and unquestioning obedience to religious gurus and community heroes. We insist on "doing our own thing," on one side of the swing, and then we desperately try to find

someone to tell us what to do. Davidman describes
this ambiguity accurately: "The modern materialist
often makes it simply: 'Do what you like' and then
rushes off to ask his psychoanalyst why he no longer
seems to like anything" (*Smoke on the Mountain*,
p. 17).

At this moment in the life of the people of Israel,
God offers a better way. At Mount Sinai both Moses
and Israel received a sign of God's grace. It is a sign of
God's will not only for Israel but also for all of
humanity. They received a practical and present-
tense sign applicable for where they were living in
their immediate situation. And through Israel this
event is to become a sign of God's grace and his will
for the earth. The sign at Mount Sinai also becomes a
key link in the total messianic portrayal and
expectation of the Old Testament; the Ten Commandments is not only a document to be heeded, but
one to stir up the human heart and mind to know the
Lawgiver behind the law.

To put it in sociological and historical terms, at
Mount Sinai, in the place of human authority and
human claims to absoluteness on the one side, and
the chaos of anarchy on the other side, a new reality
is given by God to his people in the wilderness. This
new reality will change the course of Jewish history
and the history of the world, because it is an
interruption of human society that will not be
repeated.

Moses trudges up Mount Sinai the absolute leader
of the people. He comes down from Mount Sinai
set free from his own absoluteness. In place of his
own absoluteness he is burdened by the divine

requirement and revelation of God's will. What is
new is that this revelation is documented; it is made a
part of the public record. Therefore it is quite
different from the mystical discourses Moses had
experienced at the burning bush, though the promise
of the burning bush is not thereby downgraded;
rather, it is now completed. Yahweh has spoken, and
we have the record of his speech.

Before this moment Moses alone has a direct
relationship with Yahweh. The people can only listen
dutifully to what Moses, their leader who has that
special relationship, has to say to them about his
discoveries of God's guidance. Now we see how that
is permanently altered by an event in which God
places between himself and Moses a permanently
etched self-disclosure of his will both for Moses and
the people of the Exodus. That permanent covenant
is the Ten Commandments. From now on it will be
the self-disclosure of God's will that will stand in
favor of and over against the people and also on
behalf of and over against Moses, their leader. Moses
is no longer absolute; rather, from that day onward
there is a check and a balance alongside every
sentence and every act that comes from him.

What an incredible and wonderful burden that is!
Moses is now fully responsible for everything he
does, just as the people are. For anyone who has
been to Mount Sinai, there can never be agreement
with the pernicious doctrines of "might makes
right," the "divine right of kings," or the anarchist
"rule of the jungle." From Mount Sinai onward the
law stands over the people—all of the people: the
prophet, the priest, and the king, too!

From this vantage point we are catching our first clearly focused doctrine of the dignity and worth of human beings. This is why the law is rightly described as a sign of God's grace, the covenant made at Mount Sinai. The Bible has more to say about the profound worth of human beings, but right here it is put into sharply focused outline. Our human value is put in definite and concrete terms by ten short declarations of God's will.

The law is the reason that Israel develops its rich tradition of the prophets who dare to speak out against the kings as well as against the priests and the people. It is because of this tradition of the law as God's agreement standing over Israel's life, religion, and royal leadership that the prophets are able to call out to the nation the words of both encouragement and alarm. The prophets do not create their own ethic, and from that freely chosen standpoint denounce or exhort parts of the nation that happen to offend their own particular sensitivities. They speak from a great beginning point, and, from that original self-disclosure of God to his people, they boldly call out the challenge (note Deut. 13:1-4).

The prophets of Israel, therefore, are not individualistic and eccentric religious fanatics who create causes and religious theories about which they storm their way across Israel's history. They are clear-headed interpreters of the law who point out injustice and idolatry in the land on the basis of its offense against the holy Torah of God, the roadway that Yahweh has made known. The messages of hope that the prophets announce are also rooted in the character of God as revealed in this same Torah.

This means that the prophetic tradition of Israel is a direct result of the law. Therefore it is an accurate interpretation of the history of Israel to observe that the law enables the emergence of the prophet. There are no parallels in other ancient Middle Eastern societies to this remarkable group of men and women, the prophets of Israel and Judah.

Without the existence of the Torah as the consensus document of the nation, we cannot make sense of the prophetic tradition, because that tradition is founded upon the greater criterion from which the prophet speaks and acts. Because of the mixture in Israel of law and prophets, the kings and the priests in Israel are also profoundly affected; they are not as powerful or final in their authority as their counterparts in the other societies of the ancient world. Think of it! The most powerful king of all—David—is confronted by the prophet Nathan because of David's ruthless disregard of the law of God. As Nathan tells his parable to David and comes to the conclusion of the parable, he boldly points to this awesome and popular king and announces, "You are the man. . . . Why have you despised the word of the LORD, to do what is evil in his sight?" (II Sam. 12:1-15). This is the prophetic tradition of Israel at its boldest. This confrontation is possible because the law of God calls not only the common people to repentance and the way of truth, but also the king.

But there is a certain uneasiness that exists in the relationship of the people to the law of God. This uneasiness was true of the Jews, and it is also the case among all people since the time of Moses. The mixture of feelings on our part toward the Torah might best be described as a "love-hate" relationship. On the one side, we respect the law because of its grand design and guarantee of our own worth. On the other side, the law creates its own resistance because it makes us feel our own personal and community guilt and inadequacy.

Let me give two examples to show in practical terms some of the implications of this mixture of feelings. Imagine the following situation. On the way home from a family holiday, your car has broken down late at night on the highway and you are stopped helplessly at the side of the road. You observe another car drive up behind you, and several of its occupants walk toward your car and order you to get out. You realize that you and your family are about to be the victims of a robbery—or worse. You are outnumbered; the situation is menacing. Just at that moment the flashing light of a state highway patrol car comes up alongside, having noticed your distress and the crime in progress. At such a moment you feel a deep sense of gratitude toward the law and its community representative—the peace officer, the officer of the law—because the ethical provisions of the law have become your advocate against the violence of power unchecked. Since the law is not a qualified or limited document, its protection does not favor the more powerful over the weaker. The law has ensured your worth in this dangerous moment. At such a time we cheer the law, and we are profoundly grateful for its restraining, equalizing, and humanizing effect. It has ensured our worth.

Now let me offer another story. It also tells of the flashing light of a state highway patrol car, but in the second case there is very little cheering among you or your riders in the car. You are driving along the vast reaches of the interstate highway, and this time there are no mechanical problems with the car, no helplessness at the side of the road—just the magnificent soaring thrill of high speed and top performance on the part of the car—a "state of the art" vehicle in every way! Then in the rearview mirror you catch a glimpse of the flashing light of the "Torah," and a sick feeling grips your stomach!

The Torah is the same in each instance, and the community officer played the part he was destined to play equally well in both situations, but our feelings about the law are different. The fact is that we "love" the law when it protects us from the tyrant, but we "hate" the law when we are the tyrant. We now understand how the Torah is at the same time our friend and our accuser. The law is God's kindly will toward me and in my behalf, yet it brings guilt upon me when I am the transgressor of its grand design for life.

It is essential for the study of the law in the Bible that we understand this complicated relationship toward the law that characterizes both the ancient and modern person. The technology of vehicles changes, but the crisis of the roadway remains the same.

The law has given boundaries to my life; this is its glory and its problem. Nothing will ever be the same for Moses because of this intervention. Moses is more human now, which is the good news of the law. Yet the news has its restraining effect too. It is this complicated double implication of the law that Paul chose to reflect upon in his commentary on Moses in II Corinthians 4. According to Exodus 34:29-35, we are told that Moses put a veil over his face when he came down from the mountain. Paul makes two interesting interpretive observations about this curious act by Moses. Paul tells us that Moses covered his face because he knew that the splendor of mysterious light that he had experienced high upon the mountain and was now shining from his face was in fact fading away; it was the painful fact of this "fading splendor" that Moses was hiding with his veil. In other words Moses would never again be as absolute as he once was, because from now on the people themselves have the law and Moses, their leader, is under it as much as they.

Paul's second conclusion is even more far-reaching. The law of Mount Sinai itself has a splendor that will also fade because the law cannot be finally understood apart from its fulfillment. What the law has done is stir up our guilt and our hopes so that we will not be satisfied with either until we meet the law's Author. But that is another story we will come to later.

4

The Beginning

The first words of the Ten Commandments are not the words of commandment. Before the command comes the event that stands beneath the Torah. Torah begins with the reminder to Israel of the event of redemption that chronologically preceded the words of commandment.

"And God spoke all these words, saying, 'I am the LORD your God, who brought you out of the land of Egypt, out of the house of bondage. You shall have no other gods before me' " (Exod. 20:1-3).

In the logical development of the commandments, the act of God's redemption of Israel from the bondage in Egypt is the prior fact from which the commandments as the expression of the will of Yahweh the Redeemer follow. This sequence is the fundamental beginning point of the theology of the Old and New Testaments.

Let us look at two things about that beginning point. First, notice the inseparable mixture of word and event. What God *speaks* and what God *does* are so profoundly related that we cannot successfully separate the ideology from the narratives of events in the biblical records. If the theologian attempts to develop an abstract ideological interpretation of the Torah apart from its historical roadway, the result will be an artificial and soulless document. The Torah is about living on the roadway, and it is granted to the Israelites and through them to the world by Yahweh from the very roadway of their daily life. The reason that the Torah has such universal relevance is not because it is ideologically generalized and nonspecific, but for precisely the opposite reason. The gospel of the Torah, like the gospel of its fulfillment in Jesus Christ, is universally relevant because of the historical concreteness of both events. The "eventness" is what grants to each its universal inner human persuasiveness.

When Israel is called by the Shema (Deut. 6) to remember the law, it is important to note exactly what it is that they are to remember! They are to remember the word of Yahweh and the work of Yahweh on their behalf. They were a prisoner people who were set free by the act of God, and in the wilderness that same God disclosed to Israel his will for their individual and community life.

In the same way the New Testament books are ideologically and theologically persuasive as faith documents because of the historical earnestness that shows through from writers who have witnessed a true event in the life and death and victory of Jesus of

Nazareth. It is the historical event that wins us to the gospel, not the heroic faith of the Apostles or the rhetorical eloquence of the New Testament preachers. The New Testament is convincing because the event to which it points is true.

What is most essential for us to recognize in seeking to understand both the Torah and the gospel is that the events and the messages of hope we call the Torah and the gospel are exciting documents of faith because they have their root system established in actual historical event. The law begins much earlier than the theophany of Mount Sinai. It begins at creation, at ancient Babylon when Yahweh called to Abraham to trust him, at Mount Moriah where Yahweh provided his own sacrifice in the presence of the amazed and thankful Abraham and his son Isaac. After the harrowing escape of the Jews from Egypt, the pathway was finally made ready for the disclosure of the law.

The second fact to notice is that there is theological significance to the sequence: first the act of redemption by Yahweh, then the disclosure of the divine imperative for the people. It means that the obedience of the people will be a response toward the faithfulness and love of God already revealed. It means that the great themes in the Torah—worship, ethics, and self-understanding—are values and practices that respond to what God has already shown of his own character. In biblical faith the ethical act of the believer gains its motivation from the experience of belovedness. It is not so much that we hear the command to love, but rather that our experience of the love commands us to express

toward the world the love we ourselves have already
received. Worship, self-awareness, and ethics now
become values that flow out of the prior fact of the
love and faithfulness of God.

There is one more fact about the law that is
fundamental to its understanding.

The Ten Commandments not only disclose the will
of God for human behavior, they also disclose the
divine perspective about what it means for a human
being to be human. The meaning of persons and the
meaning of community are themes of the law.
According to this portrayal in the Torah, human
personhood is understood in terms of four relationships. (1) The relationship of a human being toward
God is the first relationship portrayed in the Ten
Commandments. The first three commandments
describe that relationship. (2) The second is the
relationship with ourselves, which is implied
throughout the commandments but is in primary
focus in the fourth and fifth commandments. (3) The
next relationship, toward the neighbor, is the
primary focus of the fifth through tenth commandments. (4) The fourth relationship might be described
as our relationship toward the earth, the whole of the
created order. Each of the commandments contains
implications that come together and provide a Torah
perspective with regard to this relationship.

What we have just described might be called the
anthropology of the Ten Commandments, the
doctrine of man and woman according to the law.
The far-reaching design and intention is to portray
the will of God for his people's behavior. Therefore,
as the behavior relationships of man and woman are

described, the divine perspective concerning human beings becomes clear. Or, to put it another way, the law shows to us what God thinks of the ones to whom he grants the laws, just as an athletic coach shows his opinion of his team members by the kinds of training expectations he imposes on them. The law, therefore, reveals to us not only God's will, but also who we are according to God's total design.

The big question then is this: What specifically does that design reveal to us? It shows that we are creatures with four essential relationships—to God, ourselves, our neighbor, our earth. Put them together, and you have a human being. The implication of the law is that when any one of the four relationships is in confusion or distortion, that crisis of brokenness will gravely affect the other parts of the whole.

This interconnectedness of the four relationships is a theme of the prophets (see Isa. 1) and also of our Lord Jesus Christ in his sermon on the law (Matt. 5–7). If our ethical relationships are corrupt, that corruption will distort our relationship with God. If my relationship with God is confused and disrupted by idolatry, then that brokenness will seriously affect the way I look at myself or my neighbor or the earth. This interconnectedness is the foundation of all biblical anthropology. It means that one human being is not viewed in isolation from neighbor or earth or God.

We can now understand the strong community emphasis that is evident in the Ten Commandments and throughout the Bible. But at the same time the Ten Commandments are profoundly personal and individual. *I* am the one who must honor my parents, and *I* must worship God. *I* must find my work and my rest. This poses for me as one human being the inescapable personal challenge to stand as a unique person before God, before myself, before my neighbor, and indeed before the whole of creation.

Under the shadow of the oppression from without and the oppression from within, Israel needed the covenant of the law in order to survive. We who live in a technological age are no less in need. Malcolm Muggeridge has been a stormcrow in our time, calling out to us warnings about our own generation. In 1980 he put it dramatically in a speech at the Hoover Institute at Stanford University.

> The final conclusion would seem to be that whereas other civilizations have been brought down by attacks of barbarians from without, ours had the unique distinction of training its own destroyers at its own educational institutions and providing them with facilities for propagating their destructive ideology far and wide, all at the public expense. Thus did Western man decide to abolish himself, creating his own boredom out of his own strength, his own impotence out of his own erotomania, himself blowing the trumpet that brought the walls of his own city tumbling. And, having convinced himself that he was too numerous, labored with pill and scalpel and syringe to make himself fewer, until at last, having educated himself into imbecility and polluted and drugged himself into stupefaction, he keeled over, a weary battered old brontosaurus and became extinct.

But before judgment and extinction, we are given the chance to find the Torah and the gospel, the way of God's will, the promise of life.

5

One God

You shall have no other gods before me.

—Exod. 20:3

The Ten Commandments begin with three imperatives that have to do with our relationship to God. The first is the briefest of the three, and it makes a positive affirmation in negative terms. In this commandment we see the personal God of character set over against the false gods and the no gods. The most dramatic positive fact about this commandment is its abrupt and intense personal pronoun that becomes the key linguistic center of the commandment: "No other gods before *me*."

The holy name for God, Yahweh, which was first introduced to Moses as the personal intransitive verb "I am," "he is," becomes the name of God for Israel.

Moses is the one who heard this self-disclosure at the burning bush: "I am who I am. . . . Say this to the people of Israel, I AM hath sent me to you' " (Exod. 3:13-15). We now meet this same totally personal identification of God in the first commandment. The Ten Commandments begin on this totally personal ground: the God of character exists, and therefore no other gods can compare with the one who has revealed himself in the covenant of the law.

But this first commandment is announced to people who must live their lives in a culture that worshiped many gods. Professor von Rad insists that this central fact is an important clue to an understanding of the first commandment. "The First Commandment takes for granted a polytheistic situation amongst those who are addressed" (von Rad, *Old Testament Theology*, p. 57). The polytheistic deification of the earth was a given expectation of the period 1290 B.C. Every culture with which the Jews were familiar was polytheistic in religious outlook. The matter was simply not up for discussion in the civilizations of Egypt, Babylon, or Canaan. Therefore this commandment would be more culturally abrasive and startling in its own historical setting than in our era, which is more secular and less religious. In fact, more than a thousand years after the law of Moses, the Roman historian Tacitus will criticize the strict monotheism of the Jews as "tasteless and mean" in contrast to the other religious movements of the first century, which were more lavish and lively with fascination concerning the pantheon of gods and divine forces they embraced.

The Egyptians worship many animals and images of monstrous form; the Jews have purely mental conceptions of Deity, as one in essence. They call those profane who make representations of God in human shape out of perishable materials. They believe that Being to be supreme and eternal, neither capable of representation, nor of decay. They therefore do not allow any images to stand in their cities, much less in their temples. This flattery is not paid to their kings, nor this honour to our Emperors. From the fact, however, that their priest used to chant to the music of flutes and cymbals, and to wear garlands of ivy, and that a golden vine was found in the temple, some have thought that they worshipped Father Liber, the conqueror of the East, though their institutions do not by any means harmonize with the theory; for Liber established a festive and cheerful worship, while the Jewish religion is tasteless and mean. (*The Complete Works of Tacitus*, p. 660)

The first commandment therefore stands against the cultural expectations of 1290 B.C. This radical rejection of polytheism is drawn to its logical and most sweeping implications in the Shema of Deuteronomy 6: "Hear, O Israel: The LORD our God is one LORD, and you shall love the LORD your God with all your heart, and with all your soul, and with all your might." One God, not many! This is the teaching of the first commandment, according to the Shema.

The oneness portrayed in the Shema is personal. Pierre Teilhard de Chardin describes this intense uncompromising personhood of God as the "tenacious personalism" of holy intimacy.

To those who only know it outwardly, Christianity seems desperately intricate. In reality, taken in its main lines, it contains an extremely simple and astonishingly bold solution of the world.

In the centre, so glaring as to be disconcerting, is the uncompromising affirmation of a personal God: God as providence, directing the universe with loving, watchful care; and God the revealer, communicating himself to man on the level of and through the ways of intelligence. It will be easy for me, after all I have said, to demonstrate the value and actuality of this tenacious personalism, not long since condemned as obsolete. The important thing to point out here is the way in which such an attitude in the hearts of the faithful leaves the door open to, and is easily allied to, everything that is great and healthy in the universal. (Pierre Teilhard de Chardin, "Personalism," *The Phenomenon of Man,* pp. 292-93)

We have discovered first of all in the law that God is personal, and he is the one who can be known by human beings. Von Rad warns interpreters of the law that it is impossible to understand the Ten Commandments if we neglect this intimate, personal relationship between Yahweh and Israel (von Rad, p. 56). The opening words of the law establish this personal interpersonalness which becomes the living and integrating continuity throughout the law.

The Torah begins with the stern warning against the confusion of the human religious instinct, but there is good news within the warning. The commandment announces our freedom from the false gods and the terrors connected to them because their "bluff has been called"; the air is cleared once and for all for those who trust the commandment. The commandment is not only a warning; it is also the good news of liberation. When we trust the commandment, we are set free from the bad use of the religious instinct within each of us that searches for the lesser gods and godlike power formations to which we may give ourselves. We reach out toward ultimacy and seek to bring under our control that which we admire most and fear most. But the tragedy of religion is that practices and rituals which we ourselves create in order to establish contact with the ultimate turn sometimes silly and frivolous but too often chaotic and destructively cruel.

Because we are all incurably religious, this religious instinct with all of its imaginative possibilities needs the restraint of the first commandment. In the place of the gods and the no gods of human society, we are instead called to meet the God of character, "I am who I am," the God of event and word, the God of the covenant of the law.

This law also becomes a restraint upon the people and the practice of religion when it becomes chaotic and cruel. The horrible practice of Molech (child sacrifice), will always be understood by the Jews as against the will of God. From the time of Abraham's experience at Mount Moriah, it was overruled by God. Though that practice was common among the societies that surrounded Israel, the Jews are prohibited from such practices. When it takes place it is called an abomination. Notice how King Ahaz is described by the Old Testament historian: "Ahaz . . . did not do what was right in the eyes of the LORD. . . . He even made molten images for the Baals; and he burned incense in the valley of the son of Hinnom, and burned his sons as an offering, according to the abominable practices of the nations whom the LORD drove out" (II Chron. 28:1-3). Note also the indignation in this regard of the prophet in Isaiah 57:1-13. All religious practices of the Jews are now under the law. The zeal or sincerity of an individual in the community can no longer determine a religious practice unilaterally. The Ten Commandments stand alongside the pathway as the criteria for worship.

The prophet Isaiah, who has so profoundly challenged the idols and arrogance of the people in the early part of Isaiah 57, gives to the people the words of healing in the second half of that chapter.

> For thus says the high and lofty One
>   who inhabits eternity, whose name is Holy:
> I dwell in the high and holy place,
>   and also with him who is of a contrite and humble
>   spirit. (Isa. 57:15)

The prophet has brought the people back to the intimate and obedient relationship of the Shema by which they stand humbly before the Lord and his will.

6

Search for Meaning

> You shall not make for yourself a graven image, or any likeness of anything that is in heaven above, or that is in the earth beneath, or that is in the water under the earth; you shall not bow down to them or serve them; for I the LORD your God am a jealous God, visiting the iniquity of the fathers upon the children to the third and fourth generation of those who hate me, but showing steadfast love to thousands of those who love me and keep my commandments.
>
> —Exod. 20:4-6

The second commandment speaks directly to the problem of identity.

The word in the Old Testament Hebrew translated "graven image" becomes in the New Testament the Greek word translated "idol." In its literal sense the Greek word means shadow. The word *shadow* captures the original Old Testament force in the word

translated "graven image"—that which is projected
outward from ourselves and infused with special
religious significance. An idol, therefore, is the
attempt of a person to find and project meanings.
The creativity of human beings is shown in the idols
we have made; they show the imaginative possibilities of the human personality in that search for
meaning. The Torah is as blunt and direct in the
second commandment as in the first. We human
beings find the meaning for our existence from our
Creator Redeemer and nowhere else. In fact, when
we reach out to something else and ask or insist that
it grant this basic meaning to our lives, then we have
created an idol.

First, let us understand the theological premise
that undergirds this warning. The great presupposi-
tion of the law is found in the law's opening words.
At the very center of all reality stands the God of
character, the God identified to us by the intense
personal pronouns of the law, and by the grand "I
am who I am" disclosure to Moses at the burning
bush. The same personal intensity that Abraham and
Moses first experienced is now made known in the
law to the whole of Israel. The first commandment
with its preface, therefore, has most of all to do with
God and who he is.

In the second commandment we hear a command
that is focused more directly upon us. It directly
confronts the human need for a source from which to
make sense of life. In this commandment we discover
God's perspective on this human quest. We human
beings have been made for relationship with God
himself; therefore, to be fully human and to find out

what it means to be a man or a woman, we need to be rightly related to our creator.

Michelangelo portrayed this basic biblical principle in his profound and dramatic creation panel on the ceiling of the Sistine Chapel in Vatican City. The ceiling of this chapel, which contains one thousand square yards of frescoes, depicts nine scenes from the Old Testament. Michelangelo began this great work in 1508 and completed his part of the panels in 1511. His portrayal of the creation of Adam is a masterpiece not only because of its artistic triumph, but because it is also a theological statement about the meaning of the human creature. Michelangelo's Adam is magnificent; he has a continuity with the earth and yet with all his powerful form and majesty, his hands are empty. With one hand he is searching and reaching out for more—he knows he is incomplete. This is the portrayal of a creature who is tempted to build idols in the quest for meaning because in the whole of creation it is man and woman who yearn for the answer to "Who am I?"

Michelangelo's man is in the process of becoming human, and we are shown the moment just before God touches his frame to make him man. The gap is insurmountable; only God is able to bridge the chasm between creation and creator. The theological perspective of the artist is clear. Man does not become fully human apart from this relationship with the one who made him. What is also very clear is that when man, the human being, is touched by God, he does not become an angel or some kind of supercreature of the spiritual realm; he becomes mere man, mere woman, but made in the image of God. There is no Gnosticism in Michelangelo's portrayal; he is not describing the creation of spiritualized phantom people. The artist has painted real persons who have a continuity with the earth. There is a mystery about this man in the central panel both because of his obvious search for God and also because of God's love for him. The second commandment grants the theological foundation to that search for meaning. Both the warnings and the promises of the second commandment show how volatile is the quest and how urgent it is that the human family finds its meaning in the Lord of creation and nowhere else.

We must now ask several questions, since the commandment is so descriptive. How is it that a human being falls captive to graven images? How is it that persons and communities project onto particular objects or powers the meanings that these objects and powers do not have? How is it that a fear arises toward these graven images with such total and devastating terror as we know is the case in the worship of idols?

These questions are both very old and very contemporary. They haunt Marlow in his visit to the jungle base of Kurtz in Joseph Conrad's *Heart of Darkness*. It is the question asked by the prophet Isaiah when he looks in distress at the confusion of people who have turned their lives over to that which is false and empty: "But when I look there is no one; among these there is no counselor who, when I ask, gives an answer. Behold, they are all a delusion; their works are nothing; their molten images are empty wind" (Isa. 41:28-29).

What happens in idolatry is that persons or communities reach out toward the created order and project the strong expectations and fears that make up the essence of humanness; it is in that sense of incompleteness and in an attempt to fill in the missing whole of that incompleteness that the shadow is projected. The shadow is thereby honored by misplaced worship; it is petitioned to for benefits that it cannot fulfill. Finally, it is feared with the worst of all fear, the terror of emptiness—the yawning dark emptiness of shadows, the horror of sheer emptiness.

The second commandment makes use of the spatial cosmology of the ancient world in order to make the command communicative. "Heaven, earth, water under the earth." These levels within the created order make the command clear that nothing in any part of the created order should receive human worship or become the basis for the projected images that attempt to resemble any part of the created order. It means that the whole complex and diverse nature of the created order is included in this prohibition. There is nothing in *heaven*, that mysterious upward part of the created order (what Karl Barth calls "the creation inconceivable to us," *Dogmatics in Outline*, p. 59), that deserves human worship. Therefore to project a shadow in that direction is to seek the answer to the deepest questions from a source that is itself derivative and owes its own meanings to God.

The same warning applies to the search for meaning from the *earth*, the place of the contemporary (Karl Barth, "the creation conceivable to us,"

Dogmatics in Outline, p. 59). There are no political or
religious leaders who deserve such recognition.
When we assign to human leaders such great power
we have succeeded only in fashioning an idol
somewhat more recognizable but nevertheless still
nothing more than a relentless hollow wind.

The warning also applies to the downward side of
the cosmological mystery of creation. There are no
powers in the realms of *death* that should hold sway
over human life or conscience. This realm, frightful
as it is, is still a part of the larger whole of the created
order, and therefore is in no sense worthy of our
fears and certainly not of our worship.

Idol-making can become a very intricate process in
which a positive value like the love of the nation is
twisted into an ideal that often will justify acts of
injustice toward the neighbor who is of another
national group. This distortion of values has resulted
in the most terrifying forms of evil in our twentieth
century. Socio-religious-political idolatry has been
the graven image of the earth for each generation of
human beings; the results have been corrosive. "The
Great Masquerade of evil has played havoc with all of
our ethical concepts" (Dietrich Bonhoeffer, *Letters
and Papers from Prison,* p. 94).

The commandment identifies God as the *jealous*
God. This word is powerfully anthropomorphic; that
is, it is a word which seems humanlike in its
connotation. We should not be surprised at this
humanness, because the personalness of the Torah
has already been established in the first commandment and in the preface to the law. The word *jealous*
means to care intimately about the event taking place

so that a strong reaction is promised. God is the one who cares deeply about the events that take place, and he promises a response—either judgment or blessing. The blessing is stronger and more far-reaching—"thousands" of generations—whereas the judgment is assigned to the third and fourth generation. (The rule of Hebrew parallelism in Old Testament poetry favors this interpretation. The third and fourth generation is put alongside the parallel phrase "thousands," and we thereby may add the noun *generations* to complete the parallelism.)

What we have are two commandments and two great presuppositions of biblical faith and life that have been affirmed in the law. First the great Abrahamic and Mosaic discovery—God is personal. The second is related to the first. *We who are persons find the meaning for our existence in God and nowhere else.* The commands are stern, but they are both good news.

7

Appearance and Reality

You shall not take the name of the LORD your God in vain.

—Deut. 5:11

This commandment alerts Israel to the importance of the holy name of God. The importance of names in both the Old and New Testaments will be noted again and again. Great attention is given to names in the life of Israel. The name of a person was understood as an expression of the person's unique character.[1] Because of this cultural attention, the term *name* in the third

1. See the discussion of names and naming in Old Testament tradition in Bernhard W. Anderson's *Understanding the Old Testament*, p. 52. "In the thought of ancient Israel . . . it was believed that the name was filled with power and vitality." This helps us understand why powerful life experiences would resort in a person's being renamed (i.e., Gen. 32:27-28).

commandment is used in a highly significant sense. It is the very character and self-disclosure of Yahweh that is intended by the word *name*. We are warned not to take in vain the self-disclosure of God's character as he has made himself known to us.

The verb translated "take in vain" is the crucial term that we must make sense of in order to really understand this commandment. The most obvious meaning of this term in the Hebrew language is "to empty," or "to make empty." Professor von Rad explains, however, that another meaning lies just beneath the surface of this interesting word: "It is probable that the word which we translate as 'in vain' might at a very early period have meant 'magic' " (von Rad, p. 57).

At this point we must make a few technical observations about the study of the Ten Commandments in terms of their place in the Old Testament text. If the interpreter of the Ten Commandments agrees with the consensus of nineteenth-century Old Testament criticism and places the time of writing of these words at a late date, as, for example, the time of the prophets, then our linguistic interest from a technical standpoint is focused upon the literature and writing methods of the late or early prophetic period—from about 750 B.C. to about 400 B.C. But we now know that the Jewish language was formed and active much earlier than the form-critical scholars of the nineteenth century imagined. Therefore we are confronted with a whole new task and exciting possibility for the understanding of a document such as the Ten Commandments which, by its position in the Old Testament, claims early authorship. If in fact this document was written by Moses at or near the date 1290–1250 B.C., then we are confronted with early Hebrew vocabulary, not late Hebrew. *YHWH* (Yahweh), therefore, is understood as an old word, not as the linguistic invention of prophetic writers.

This shift in balance in Old Testament linguistic study has produced a whole new interest in the formation and development of the Hebrew language. The recent archaeological discoveries at Ebla, at Tell Mardikh in Syria, are of tremendous importance in this inquiry because they have given to scholars the opportunity to search out some examples of early, concrete, daily-use meanings of Hebrew words. These, in addition to other archaeological evidences of early Semitic literacy, such as the Sumerian prism and the Code of Hammurabi, have moved all dates for Old Testament authorship to earlier periods. The traditional Jewish understanding of the authorship of Old Testament books is now more reasonable and faithful to the evidence than most of the elaborate theories that were dogmatically asserted by the form-critical scholars of the nineteenth and early twentieth centuries. Those critics who dominated Old Testament studies with their dismissal of the possibility of Mosaic authorship of the books of the law have now been strongly challenged.

In my opinion, because of the scholarly dismissal of the Torah as a genuine document from the Mosaic period of the Exodus, interpreters who have followed that direction have not seriously encountered the text of the Ten Commandments as a literary whole. Form criticism has as its goal the interpretation of the text in terms of its historical setting and in particular the religious atmosphere, setting, and needs of the community from which the text arose. But what happens in practice in much of the form-critical method is that the biblical text is read through the filter of the modern scholar's assessment of what constitutes the probable historical-religious needs of the ancient community within which we find the document. When it is careful and modest, form criticism of a biblical text is a useful research tool. But as we can demonstrate unhappily in many examples of Old and New Testament textual studies, the form-critical method of interpretation has often become so imaginative and inventive on the part of the scholar that the text is not allowed to simply speak for itself. We who are doing the interpretation often exaggerate the cultural, religious evidence that we find theologically interesting or useful to our own theological goals. The text is then brought under the control of alien criteria, under the mistaken notion that we have discovered a stratum of material or ancient influence that was at work on the material.

The documentary hypothesis of the Pentateuch had this kind of negative influence upon the study of the Decalogue. The search for strands of influence effectively blocked the consideration of the Ten Commandments as a single literary whole. Yet it is clear from the standpoint of literary criticism that Israel had the document as a whole. This is the point of its actual position in Exodus 20 and Deuteronomy 5.

Let me offer an extreme example of how far-fetched such form-critical research methods can become, and perhaps even show how a few faulty premises as to the true weight of evidence lead to total misunderstanding.

George Gershwin wrote the symphonic work *Rhapsody in Blue* on commission to be played by Paul Whiteman and his orchestra at the dedication of the Aeolian Music Hall of New York in 1924, with Gershwin himself at the piano. But isn't such a statement all too simple? A form critic would insist upon the examination of Gershwin's composition at a much deeper socio-historical level. The key to this interpretive study for the form critic rests in the piece's community expectation and the requirement for a music hall dedication composition.

This examination, in fact, is the first error in judgment by the form critic. But notice how far this initial premise might possibly take us. We must make an exhaustive sociological and religious motivation study of the Brooklyn Music Hall Board of Governors who commissioned the original work. We discover that Peter Steinway, a member of the committee and a strong supporter of the use of pianos, made at least four telephone calls to Gershwin. This discovery conclusively establishes what we will term the *piano strata* in the final work. The Paul Whiteman faction cannot be discounted, nor can the strong community percussionist faction. The members of the Brooklyn Drum Corps had made several successful tours during the previous year, 1923, and through their representative on the Board of Governors, they were exerting strong percussionist influence upon the composer and his circle. Some interpreters have argued for the Al Jolson melody theory, since he and Gershwin had earlier worked together on "Swanee."

Our conclusion from this examination is, therefore, that *Rhapsody in Blue* is not so much Gershwin, though we must admit that New Yorkers popularly assigned it to him, as it is really Brooklyn ceremony music of the period 1920–24. Some scholars even propose that Gershwin himself may have actually written the middle fourteen measures that embellish the Jolson theme prior to the Steinway intrusion.

Such an interpretive approach to *Rhapsody in Blue* misunderstands it because the study began with a faulty premise. The most important task and the first task for all concerned is to listen to the music as a whole. The other research is valid and possibly useful, but it is literary criticism, or rather music criticism in this case—the study of the text itself as it stands in the larger text—that is the essential beginning place. The clues to the music still belong to the music itself.

This is why literary criticism is a much more basic beginning place for Bible study than form criticism. We must first of all listen to the text as it speaks in its own terms. This means that we must study the particular text of the Old or New Testament first of all as it is presented to us in its own context.

What does all of this mean for our study of the word choice "in vain" in the third commandment? It means that this word is old, and we therefore want to face its old meanings as well as its later meanings. In its later development the word carries the sense of "empty." We are commanded against any carelessness on our part toward the holy meaning of who

God is in his personhood; such carelessness might
lead us into emptying the holy name of God of its
content. We know from von Rad's research into the
older period of the Hebrew word that it also carries
within it the sense of "magic." This means that the
third commandment warns against the vanity not
only of emptiness but also of sorcery and magic. Both
kinds of vanity are destructive because both diminish
the name of the Lord.

Now let us look more closely at the word. *Shw* is
the Hebrew word, and its concrete root meaning is
"empty pit." This word is also the word for "ruin,"
"devastation." One of the verb forms of this word
means to pervert, to ruin, to make something empty.
An interesting use of this word is found in I Samuel
28:3-9, where the witch of Endor is described as
having the spirit of the "hollow sound." This same
word, *shw*, is the word that now appears in the third
commandment.

How are we to understand the commandment?
First, we are commanded not to pervert or profane
the name of the Lord. This is what happens when the
good name of God is reversed so that the name of
love becomes the means of curse. What happens in
profanity is that the name of the holy and righteous
God is used as a term of ruin and devastation.
Someone or something is damned by the name of the
holy one who was first identified to us as the
Redeemer! What an ironic twist and perversion!

We are also commanded not to empty the name of
God with the hollow flattery of adoration which is
not matched by the relationship of discipleship.
The name is used and even honored—at least

apparently—but the praise is actually emptied by the unwillingness to act out the words we speak. This emptying is the milder form of the word *shw*, but it can be equally destructive because of its built-in self-deception. We are tempted to think that because we have spoken the words we have therefore done what we have spoken. Jesus put it this way in his own commentary on the law: "Not every one who says to me Lord, Lord shall enter the kingdom of heaven, but he who does the will of my Father" (Matt. 7:21).

We are also commanded not to practice sorcery or any form of magic arts, though they may be designed to enable us to make contact with God or with some other spiritual reality. They, like the counsel of the witch of Endor, are the counsel of the "hollow sound." We have no need of the magician or religious guru because God is able to speak for himself.

Now the question we must, therefore, ask is this. If we are not to empty the name of the Lord in any of these three ways, then what are we to do? What is the opposite of "to empty"? The psalm of the law, Psalm 119, faces this very question by its practical affirmations.

> Teach me, O LORD, the way of thy statutes;
>   And I will keep it to the end.
> Give me understanding, that I may keep thy law
>   and observe it with my whole heart.
> Lead me in the path of thy commandment,
>   for I delight in it.
> Incline my heart to thy testimonies,

and not to gain!
Turn my eyes from looking at vanities;
   and give me life in thy ways.
Confirm to thy servant thy promise,
   which is for those who fear thee.
Turn away the reproach which I dread;
   for thy ordinances are good.
Behold, I long for thy precepts;
   in thy righteousness give me life!
Let thy steadfast love come to me, O LORD,
   thy salvation according to thy promise. (Ps. 119:33-41)

Joy Davidman has caught the essence of this psalm and the positive intention of the third commandment in her comments on this commandment. She states it in positive terms: "Thou shalt take the Name of the Lord thy God in earnest! . . . It is high time" (*Smoke on the Mountain*, p. 47).

Now let us review the three great theological presuppositions with which the Torah begins.

First, we meet the God of character who can be known and loved because he is the one who first redeemed Israel. He is the one personal God.

Second, we are confronted with the fact that the meaning of existence is to be found in God himself and nowhere else.

Third, God is the one who discloses his own character and makes himself known. He speaks for himself and therefore we have no need for magicians or our own empty phrases. We have only to earnestly listen.

8

The Balanced Life

Observe the sabbath day, to keep it holy, as the LORD *your God commanded you. Six days you shall labor, and do all your work; but the seventh day is a sabbath to the* LORD *your God; in it you shall not do any work, you, or your son, or your daughter, or your manservant, or your maidservant, or your ox, or your ass, or any of your cattle, or the sojourner who is within your gates, that your manservant and your maidservant may rest as well as you. You shall remember that you were a servant in the land of Egypt, and the* LORD *your God brought you out thence with a mighty hand and an outstretched arm; therefore the* LORD *your God commanded you to keep the sabbath day.*

—Deut. 5:12-15

The word *sabbath* in this text is one of the few Hebrew words that have been transliterated directly into English usage without translation. The three other most well-known words are *hallelujah*, which translates as "praise the Lord"; *hosanna*, which translates as "please help"; and *amen*, which means "faithful." *Sabbath* is the Hebrew root for several Old Testament words. Its literal meaning is "cease," but it is also a root word for words translated "seven" and "rest."

The presentation of this commandment in Deuteronomy contains several sentences not found in the Exodus text. "You shall remember. . . ." This added sentence more concretely unites the fourth commandment to the first commandment and to the preface. The Exodus text of the fourth commandment relates the sabbath commandment to creation; the Deuteronomy text relates it to redemption.

Again we must ask the question, What is the meaning of this commandment? What does it teach us about life in addition to what it commands?

It is important to notice that this commandment offers an interpretation of the ordinary day-to-day living of human beings and the world they occupy. A unit of time, namely seven days, is used as a framework within which we are able to think about ourselves and our work, relationship, worship, rest. Man and woman are not assessed in terms of their relationship to a year or a month or a day but to a week. Not only that, but the week is understood in terms of an intrinsic rhythm of work and rest.

What does this description of the human being and his or her world teach? From it we learn that we are so designed that we need to work and to rest, to act and to be, to run and to walk. The portrayal is rhythmic, and human life is pictured within the context of an essential balance.

We are creatures who need to stop and think, to worship and rest. We need unhurried time within the balance of the seven ordinary days in order to collect our thoughts and to remember who we are. We need to remember the fact of the goodness of creation and the redemptive love that has been granted to us. The Torah interpretation of personhood includes this rhythmic week as an essential ingredient of humanness. It is presented not as a desirable possibility for the affluent but as the essential mark for all humankind, and therefore it is mandated.

In other words, from the perspective of the Torah we human beings are designed to live a rhythmic week; we function best in the wise and good rhythm of work and rest, time alone and time in community, intensive experiences and extensive experiences, physical exercise and mental exercise. This is the view of life that is being taught in the commandment.

In the context of this seven-day framework, it becomes the role of the fourth commandment to affirm the universal relevance of the law. The essential balance of the rhythmic week is God's gift not only for the benefit of the rich person but also for the slave, not only for men but also for women, not only for Jewish citizens but also for sojourners (foreigners), not only for the human family in creation, but also for animals.

In the later extension of the law, this rhythmic principle will be applied in many directions. For example, the land itself will benefit from this commandment: "For six years you shall sow your land and gather in its yield; but the seventh year you shall let it rest and lie fallow, that the poor of your people may eat; and what they leave the wild beasts may eat" (Exod. 23:10-11). Institutions are to be rhythmic as well as, for example, the concept of the jubilee year after seven times seven years (Lev. 25).

The law has in its way paid to man and woman and the created order they occupy a rich compliment. We human beings are not mechanical, timeless creatures that can grind on endlessly at work. We need quality time to collect our thoughts and our dreams. We need time to "cease" and to wonder about the deep meanings of life. We need to remember our history and to worship the Lord of life. Though the fourth commandment is an imperative, it is an imperative that leads us toward freedom.

It also leads to dominion. In the earliest chapters of the Bible (Gen. 1:26), man and woman are granted dominion over the earth, and this dominion text becomes the beginning of the freedom theology of the Bible. Now, in the fourth commandment of the law, that dominion thread is once again affirmed. The fourth commandment tells us to choose the good way within the seven-day cycle that describes our lives. We chose the work and we chose the rest, and we are given dominion over the mandate. We are to find our work and to find our rest; that is to say, we are given the responsibility to think through the meaning of our life within the seven days each of us has to live this week. The commandment is therefore concerned with the positive framework of work and rest given by God through men and women as a gift to the created order for our good.

During his ministry Jesus confronted more confusion and antagonism concerning the fourth commandment than all the rest of the law. Most of that confusion and opposition centered upon the meaning of the gift of the "cease" day, the day of rest. Ironically, this gift had become a misunderstood and totally legalized battlefield of argument and stress by the time of the first century. The Essenes would prove their own ascetic superiority over the Pharisees by insisting upon more stringent "cease" regulations than the Pharisee lawyers could justify.[1] This law of the good balance had become so much the technical specialty of the religious lawyers that most of its ethical richness and human atmosphere had been contaminated by self-righteous one-upmanship. Jesus does not hesitate to challenge this serious distortion of the gospel intention of the Torah. One of the most dramatic confrontations concerning the fourth commandment is recorded for us by Mark.

Again he entered the synagogue, and a man was there who had a withered hand. And they watched him, to see whether he would heal him on the sabbath, so that they might accuse him. And he said to the man who had the withered hand, "Come here." And he said to them,

1. An example of this is found in Jesus' challenge to the Pharisees in Matthew 12:11 concerning the man who helped a lamb out of a pit on the sabbath. This question points up a difference of extremity between Pharisee interpreters and the hard-line sabbatarianism of the Qumran sect. The Qumran sect held, "No one should help an animal to foal on the sabbath day. And if it should drop [its foal] into a pit or well, let not one raise it on the sabbath day" (H. H. Rowley, "Zadokitework," in *From Moses to Qumran*, p. 251).

"Is it lawful on the sabbath to do good or to do harm, to save life or to kill?" But they were silent. And he looked around at them with anger, grieved at their hardness of heart and said to the man, "Stretch out your hand." He stretched it out, and his hand was restored. The Pharisees went out, and immediately held counsel with the Herodians against him, how to destroy him. (Mark 3:1-6)

Notice how Jesus focuses attention upon the goodness of the fourth commandment and its beneficent purpose. The tragedy of this narrative is that his listeners are firmly entrenched in their own legalism and fear. The result of the anxious technical fascination with the correct definition of *work* and *rest* is a hardness and joylessness that is totally foreign to the generous design of the commandment.

The other half of the rhythm is work; six days we are to work. The logic of the commandment is clear; rest without work is nonrhythmic just as work without rest is nonrhythmic. Each needs its companion gift in order to be truly humanizing. When work and rest are united, we have a stewardship view of life. The fourth commandment looks at our individual lives and the lives of the created order that surround us in terms of health and balance. This commandment grants to us the dominion, the responsibility, for care of ourselves and the earth. We are not to exploit ourselves on the earth or those who work for us, but we are to do good by the tasks of our work and by the reflective pauses of our rest. The doctrine of work brings us into a dynamic and creative relationship with the earth as we make use of the unique giftedness in our stewardship responsibility. The six days of work earn the money to support the family and good works, and make it possible for the family to rest. There is an economic balance as well as a psychological and sociological balance.

But work is work and there is no easy way to work, whether it is feeding livestock, learning complicated mathematical equations, doing serious Bible study, or typing manuscripts. For some people there is no easy way to rest either—but work is still harder because it lasts longer (at least during our lifetime). There are six days of work to the one day of rest in the balanced week of our earthly existence. Work is good and it has many spiritual and physical benefits, but work by definition is hard.

This past year I had a conversation with three wranglers who were in charge of the horses at one of the InterVarsity Ranch camps in Alberta, Canada. We were talking about the horses and the very cold weather of Alberta during the winter. I made the unknowing observation, "You keep the horses in barns during the winter months, don't you?"

The wranglers enjoyed the next few minutes telling me that, quite to the contrary, the horses stayed outside during the winter. "We have trees on the range where they keep out of the worst wind."

I was amazed and followed up my first question with what I thought was a reasonable second question: "But you don't ride them in the winter, do you?"

They were also cheered by this question as they assured me that the horses loved to be ridden in the winter at below-zero temperatures. One final sentence really struck me. "Of course, after every ride it is very important to walk them around and completely wipe them down so their sweat doesn't chill them."

It was then I realized that wrangling horses at thirty degrees below zero was hard work, and not everyone was up to it. Perhaps it has been the western films that have made a cowboy's life seem so carefree and almost casual. The fact is that all work is very hard some of the time. Nevertheless, if it is honest work it should be good. "Sweat is one thing that money can't buy."

A good criterion pervades the fourth commandment. The good result of work, in addition to the task completed, is that through hard work we are enabled to develop our full stride as human beings. It is at work where a young man or a young woman develops the skills and talents of his or her uniqueness. Both rest and work help us to feel good about ourselves, not only about our *hearts* but also about our *hands,* not only about what we think and feel but also about what we do.

A rhythmic stride emerges from work and rest that confirms our humanness, and that stride should continue throughout our lives until the day we die. The Bible does not have a doctrine of retirement; rather what it has is a doctrine of discipleship with variations in the kinds of work and rest we are to choose and do. It is harmful to superimpose upon people an artificial expectation that at a certain arbitrary age they should "retire" and from that point on live nonrhythmically. Such an expectation is dangerous to mental and spiritual health, and even physical health. We are to work and to rest in rhythmic balance, if possible, right up to the end of our lives. The work may perhaps evolve through several fascinating careers and opportunities of stewardship and service, but work and rest must accompany each other throughout the journey.

The commandment lays the responsibility upon each one of us directly and personally. We must find our work and find our rest. Some persons develop the expectation that others force them to rest or in some cases force them to work. The commandment does not encourage such an expectation. As a pastor, I often meet parishioners who will say to me, "I am willing to be of service, but no one in the church has asked me to help out." But to these people the text says, "You must find your work; it is there to do; if you do not find it, it is your problem." The point of the commandment is that a stewardship obligation is being affirmed. Other people I meet are, by choice, workaholics, and are sometimes secretly proud of the fact that they have mercilessly burned the candles of their lives at every place a wick was visible. But the commandment lays upon them the obligation to balance their lives for the good of the earth and for their own good.

Though this fact of inescapable personal obligation is true in the commandment, it is also true that one of the finest gifts we can share with other human beings is to help them find their work and their balance between rest and work. When young people are enabled to get started in the working world, a sub-stantial contribution has been made toward their

sense of well-being. Self-confidence is greatly in-
fluenced by how a person succeeds in the working
half of the rhythm. The fourth commandment does
not attach an inordinate importance to work as the
indicator of worth or personal significance; rather, it
places weight upon the principle of wholeness. We
have here the beginnings of a shalom theology, the
theology of health and integration which we will
reflect upon in greater detail as the total shape of the
law comes into clearer focus.

We must now develop two more theological
themes that are important ingredients of the fourth
commandment. First, this commandment shows us
that nothing goes on and on without interruption.
There are limits built into God's design for our life,
our authority, and our responsibility. This commandment treats life in terms of a concrete boundary;
the segment of seven days has a beginning and an
ending because of God's good decision. The boundary which limits our work is not a punishment but
has the same kind of theological significance as the
Genesis portrayal of six days of creation. Each day is
drawn to a close and is considered by the stated
opinion of God—"it is good." It is good that history
has boundaries; it is good that our work fits within a
context of meaning. It is good that God's decision
stands at the beginning and at the end.

But the most profound truth hidden within this
commandment has to do with the meaning of the
seventh day as a sign of the movement of human
history toward the messianic fulfillment of history.
The seventh day concludes the week in the same way
as in the grand account of creation—the seventh day

is the day without an ending, the day that belongs to God, on which he rested. From a theological viewpoint this may explain why our Lord consciously and deliberately asserted his own authority over the day of rest in the fourth commandment. Jesus concludes one debate with the Pharisees concerning the proper observation of the sabbath with the bold sentence, "I tell you, something greater than the temple is here. . . . For the Son of man is Lord of the sabbath" (Matt. 12:1-8).

St. Augustine was convinced that the real significance of the sabbath is this fact, that it provided a concrete sign of fulfillment toward which history yearns; because of the grace and decision of God, human history moves toward that fulfillment symbolized by the seventh day. He opened and concluded his *Confessions* with variations on this thought: "Thou madest us for thyself, and our heart is restless until it repose in thee" (p. 3). "O Lord God, give peace unto us . . . the peace of rest, the peace of the Sabbath, which hath no evening . . . thou, Lord, ever workest, and art ever at rest" (p. 337).

There is the rhythm—"ever at work, ever at rest." God's meaning in Jesus Christ has permanently changed everything for the better: "Do little things as though they were great, because of the majesty of Jesus Christ who does them in us, and who lives our life; and do the greatest things as though they were little and easy, because of His omnipotence" (Pascal, *Pensées*, #552).

9

Honor Thy Father and Mother

Honor your father and your mother, that your days may be long in the land which the LORD your God gives you.

—Exod. 20:12

The word *honor* is the essential word in understanding the fifth commandment. The Hebrew word *coben* means in its most literal sense "to weigh heavy." This is the word for "precious," "valuable." The Septuagint writers chose the Greek word *timaō* for the Septuagint translation. In classical Greek *timaō* carries this same meaning, "of great value or worth," and as a verb, "to set a high value upon." The question for us is this: What does this word mean as it is used in the commandment?

Taken in its most basic sense, we discover in the fifth commandment that it is God's will for us that we weigh our parents heavy, that we recognize their great worth. The command is not conditional; it is sheer gospel! We are to give the gift of honor to our parents; they are to be weighed heavy. We ourselves have already been "weighed heavy" by God, a fact which the opening preface of the first commandment of the law has made clear to us. We were called to remember that redemption gift in the fourth commandment, and now we are exhorted to share that gift of belovedness in the relationships around us. The horizontal movement of the law's ethical implications begins with our own parents.

Unlike the commands that will follow, the fifth commandment states positively what we *are* to do instead of negatively what we are *not* to do. The apostle Paul draws attention to the fact that there is a promise sentence attached to this commandment: "that your days may be long in the land which the LORD your God gives you" (note Eph. 6:2). Though Paul draws attention to this commandment's promise, it is also true that in the Old Testament the promise of blessing accompanies the entirety of the law and not only this single commandment. The Deuternomy text that precedes the restatement of the whole law makes this plain. "And now O Israel, give heed to the statutes and the ordinances which I teach you, and do them; that you may live. . . . Keep them and do them; for that will be your wisdom and your understanding in the sight of the peoples, who, when they hear all these new statutes, will say, 'Surely this great nation is a wise and understanding people.' For what great nation is there that has a God so near to it as the LORD our God is to us"

(Deut. 4:1-7). What we do have in the promise of the
fifth commandment is another restatement of the
promise of blessing from the God who is very near to
Israel in his love. The blessing covers and accompanies the whole law but is now specifically
emphasized in connection with this commandment.

The fifth commandment contains a mandate that is
not only an encouragement to fathers and mothers
but contains an unmistakable challenge to them as
well. We who are parents are grateful to hear the
good advice that is being given to our children, but,
as we ponder the full meaning of the word *honor*, we
are also deeply challenged by the mandate to ask
several questions of ourselves. One is, "How heavy
am I?"—not in the "weight-watcher" sense, but in
that deeper sense of the will of God for my life. When
I am weighed, how substantial is my life as a parent,
friend, and model to my children? Though the
commandment does not invite families to apportion
the degree of honor on the basis of some particular
honor—some weight criterion—because no criterion
is offered in the commandment, nevertheless the
word *honor* itself is so good and so rich in its intrinsic
meaning that it draws out of me in a friendly way this
inevitable introspection and inner self-evaluation.

It is most important, it seems to me, for us to grasp
that this commandment at its core presents to us a
gospel understanding of life. That way of looking at
life begins in the way we look at those closest to
us—our mothers and our fathers. What we have
established here is the ethical atmosphere within
which all ethical teaching concerning the neighbor
will benefit. Ethics in the law and the prophets will

share that same atmosphere. We love others from the richness that comes from God's prior act in our behalf through which he redeemed us and honored us. From that event-resource we are given the mandate to love those who are around us. The practice of evaluation is not made a part of the commandment. The question, "Does this parent deserve honor from children?" is not inserted into the mandate as a qualifier. The parents are to be honored because God has granted them this gift which is to be received through their children. The children are the bearers of a gift from God to their parents.

There is a dynamic and living nature about this commandment, and the promise of the commandment spells it out in terms of life—"that your days may be long." The Deuteronomy 5 text also adds, "and that it may go well with you." In other words, there is a good effect that results from the ethical relationship in which one human being is honored—weighed heavy—by another human being. Out of that gift grows a tremendous encouragement force, setting loose energy. The gift of honor has the practical impact of helping the person who is honored to live up to this positive assessment of his or her worth. We are standing once again at the gospel core of the Torah in the same way as we were at the law's beginning. This center will come to its own fulfillment at the cross of Jesus Christ, where all of humanity is invited to make the ultimate discovery of how heavy every one of us has been weighed by God. "God shows his love for us in that while we were yet sinners Christ died for us" (Rom. 5:8).

There is dynamic motivational power in the experience of such honor. This fact has been demonstrated in educational research. In one experiment it was found that teachers who were told the children in their classrooms were "gifted" had more success in the classroom and achieved higher results than would be expected from the children's test scores. In sharp contrast it was demonstrated that in classroom situations where teachers were told that their students were "slow" (though in fact in the control testing situation, IQ scores showed the students to be equal in status), the learning and achievement results were lower.

This classroom research has demonstrated that when someone is "weighed light" to us, we treat such a person with lower expectations. Unless, therefore, the teacher in such a setting is determined to prove the preliminary evaluation wrong, the student will usually sink to the lower, slower track to which he or she has been weighed. This is one factor that produces learned failure among children. On the other hand, the student who is not weighed light by teachers and family is encouraged toward greater achievement and self-confidence.

This powerful force is one of the thematic threads Meredith Willson has skillfully drawn out through his brilliant musical play *The Music Man*. "Professor" Harold Hill is certainly a con artist even by his own admission, but when we look more closely at what is really happening in River City, Willson has proved his title true. Harold Hill is a music man; he sees possibilities where others did not.

Tommy Djlis is a town ruffian who is always called by Mayor Shinn "ya wild kid ya," but Harold Hill sees Tommy as a leader, and in fact Professor Hill appoints him as the band leader of the River City Boys' Band. All of this confidence has a transforming impact upon Tommy. The fact is that Professor Hill weighed the boy heavier than did the rest of the citizens.

Winthrop is a very shy and defeated lad who has such a serious stuttering problem that he almost refuses to talk. Members of his family have given in to his problem, and, though they love him, they have agreed to protect him from the demands of talking; in effect, they talk for him. But Professor Hill sells him a trumpet and even teaches him to sing a song which he has convinced Winthrop has practically no s's at all. Winthrop sings "Gary, Indiana" to his amazed family with almost no trouble. But what is so exciting and what makes it such a great show song is that for this boy who thought he could not speak his s's, Professor Hill has sneaked in quite a few, all the way from "syncopation" to "home sweet home."

I am convinced that C. S. Lewis is correct in the point he makes in his remarkable speech "The Weight of Glory" that the cure for pride is not the humiliation of a person so that pride is broken. Rather, the cure for pride is to honor people so that they do not need the false support of a proud spirit. "I suddenly remembered that no one can enter heaven except as a child; and nothing is so obvious in a child—not a conceited child, but a good child—as its great and undisguised pleasure in being praised" (*The Weight of Glory*, p. 9).

The fifth commandment is interpreted in a direct way by the apostle Paul in his Letter to the Ephesians. Since the Apostle expands its logical implications, I think it is important for our study to examine the way in which Paul interprets this commandment. Paul includes his interpretation in the context of a series of ethical, interpersonal statements of advice to the Christians at Ephesus.

> Children, obey your parents in the Lord, for this is right. "Honor your father and mother" (this is the first commandment with a promise), "that it may be well with you and that you may live long on the earth." Fathers, do not provoke your children to anger, but bring them up in the discipline and instruction of the Lord. (Eph. 6:1-4)

Notice that Paul draws the commandment into a full-circle argument. As children are expected to honor parents, so with equal importance parents are to honor children. The two halves of the circle cannot be separated from each other. A broken-spirited child does not know how to honor, because the word *honor* implies a decision that is made, and a human being must be taught and encouraged and set free in order to be able to make decisions. Paul has combined the two halves of the circle into one whole.

Paul also introduces a word not found in the fifth commandment language. It is the word *obey.* "Children, obey your parents . . ." The word behind Paul's Greek word is an Old Testament word that is profoundly connected in the Jewish mind with the law; it is the Hebrew word *shema*, "hear." Jewish

worship begins with that very word, "Hear, O
Israel." Paul tells the children that they should hear
their parents. This word does not replace the word
honor, but rather it is a logical implication to be drawn
from it. *Honor* is still the larger word.

Obey has two meanings. In its narrower sense it
means to strictly follow instructions, to submit
without argument. In its broader sense *shema* and its
Greek counterpart in the Ephesian sentence have the
meaning of "hear, listen closely because of the deep
relationship."

It is important for the interpreter to recognize that
the word *obey* becomes rich and meaningful as it is
enveloped within the larger contextual word of the
commandment—*honor*. Another way to explain this
difference is to watch how the words relate in the
child-parent journey through life. *Honor* never alters,
whereas the word *obey* goes through a grand cycle of
continuous change. *Obey* as a human experience of a
child begins in infancy and early childhood as total
submission. The very survival of a small child
depends upon the protection and care of parents;
therefore, the instructions about streets and medi-
cine cabinets are nonnegotiable and must be obeyed.
The narrowest definition of *obey* must apply in the
earliest period of a child's life. But the word *obey* is a
dynamic word, and its meaning alters through the
journey of growing up. It moves through the
"straining at the boundaries" period of youth and
adolescence. Finally, in the independent years of
adulthood, the roles may be completely reversed as
the older parent is in a situation where he or she
obeys the children and follows their advice. The

obedience roles are basically fluid so that they are in
continuous change, much to the benefit of both
children and parents. For example I am the one who
taught each of my three children to ski downhill, and
at this writing I am still a valuable instructor to my
youngest. But as a matter of fact my older two
children have already become my teachers, and I
listen very closely when they speak. Yet notice that
throughout the dynamic transformation of the
obedience experience in life, the larger word *honor*
has stayed the same. We must always weigh heavy
our father and our mother.

Two other important theological ingredients are
present in this commandment. Just as we observed in
our study of the fourth commandment, we are given
in the fifth commandment one more reminder that
has profound theological importance. We as human
beings are seen not in isolation but as a part of a
continuity of the generations. We therefore need our
parents, and parents need their children, not only for
who they are to us, but because they link us to our
roots and to the future. The human personality needs
both of these essential dimensions in order to
describe itself and its unique identity. It is necessary
for the child growing up to hear the stories and
traditions that enrich self-understanding, and it is
equally important for adults to project themselves
toward the future. Think of it! The young couple who
have a baby in 1984 have projected their concerns and
obligations deep into the twenty-first century. This is
one of the vital roles that the Christian church has
to fulfill as it offers a transgenerational extended
family to adults and children, so that children without

grandparents nearby can borrow from the congregation men and women who can become loving partners with them in their linkage to the tradition of the past. In the same way the fellowship offers the opportunity for single adults to invest their lives and creative energy into the lives of children.

Recently I met a husband and wife in their late fifties. They had discovered that as their children had grown up and moved away from the family home, they were increasingly becoming an "evening at the TV" couple. A friend invited them to attend a Young Life Club meeting of high school teenagers. In a very brief time this couple had become adult sponsors to the Young Life Club at the high school their own children had attended. I really enjoyed one comment that this man made to me. "You know I only work to support my Young Life habit." This couple had decided to invest continually in the next generation of human beings in their city; they borrowed children now that their own had grown up.

One other important fact to notice is that the relationship of parents and children is not treated as a private relationship. An intervention has taken place within the intimate and privileged relationship called the family. The law expresses to us the will of God; now we have discovered that God's will for life knows no privacy barriers. In his restatement of the law in the Letter to the Ephesians, Paul uses an important phrase to make this fact dramatically clear. Paul encourages children to "obey your parents in the Lord, for this is right" (Eph. 6:1). The phrase "in the Lord" is the key phrase. The relationship of children and parents is mediated by the Lord Jesus

Christ. In other words there is a greater context within which the relationship of fathers, mothers, and children must find its meaning.

Dietrich Bonhoeffer develops this very important theological point in his book *The Cost of Discipleship*. He maintains that because of Jesus Christ we do not have direct relationships with people; instead, we have mediated relationships. "Jesus Christ stands between us and God, and for that very reason he stands between us and all other men and things. *He is the mediator,* not only between God and man, but between man and man" (p. 85).

That good mediation was begun by the words of the law, preparing the way for the personal mediation of the Lord of the law. This means that the community is also involved in our families. The law has made it clear that what happens between children and their parents is a part of the concern of the people of the Torah. Therefore a battered youngster who is beaten by a mother or father must be the concern of the community. In the same way parents under threat from children are to be the concern of the community. It is necessary for the community to exercise its responsibility in order to protect the family from the marauder who, in these instances, is within the family itself. The fifth commandment has honored the oldest institution in the human created order by this good intervention.

We all have a stake in the health of families, so much so that the society itself will suffer as the family suffers. But our stake as a community must be toward the goal expressed by the Torah—toward a healthy and weighed-heavy relationship between parents and children. This means clearly established guidelines and restraints are implied within the commandment toward the society as it seeks to be helpful toward the family. The community must have the same goal as the Torah in its ministry toward parents and children.

Nor is the community, in any sense, an adequate replacement for the family. The commandment does not say "Children, honor your commune." The mandate is clear—"Honor your father and mother." The law describes a highly personal three-way relationship for each human being—father, mother, child—and the community must be very cautious about tampering with that profoundly important human intimacy. Egalitarian and community objectives are no substitute for the intention of this commandment. Where this primary intimacy is eroded because of powerful community pressure either religious or secular, the results are harmful; the human personality needs the basic triad described by the fifth commandment.

It is not surprising that one of the most common characteristics of cultic religious movements and totalitarian political movements is to consciously and carefully redirect this vast word *honor*, which has blessed the fifth commandment, toward either the religious or the political community. Cultic and totalitarian movements have recognized that it is too dangerous to allow human beings to have in their own hands such a dynamically powerful gift as the word *honor* implies. Therefore the movement that has as its goal the management and control of people must find ways to interfere with the relationships within the family so that the family becomes effectively submissive to the goals of the movement.

The Ten Commandments, however, do not interfere with this privacy. Though the law handles our relationships, the intervention of both the law and the gospel enriches the freedom and the intimacy of the family because of the greater context into which the family has been set. The commandment offers a whole theological framework for existence, not a human system whether religious or political. When Jesus Christ, as the Lord of the law and the gospel, is the center of the family, then the source of meaning, of forgiveness, of hope, of love becomes the rock upon which we build our foundations of family commitment and love.

The family, therefore, is set upon a double foundation: our own love and faithfulness toward each other, and God's love and faithfulness as the solid rock beneath our commitment. When we agree to the law and the gospel, we acknowledge that double foundation; we accept God's intervention as good.

Just as circumcision was a sign of this intervention covenant for the synagogue of the Old Testament, so the baptism of infants is the sign of our agreement to this intervention in the New Testament church. During the baptism, the parents release their infant daughter or son to the pastor for the few moments in which the child receives the mark of water and the gift of his or her Christian name as a child of the covenant. When the mother or father takes the child back, something of great importance has been acted out. We have claimed the love and faithfulness of

God toward our child just as we do in all of our prayers; we have ourselves, with the fellowship of the church in agreement, promised our own faith and covenant; but we have also admitted publicly that this small life in our family is not our possession or even the extension of our existence. This young human being is a unique person beloved by God with his or her worth guaranteed by God's prior decision and act. Just as prayer does not create God's love, but responds to God's love, so baptism acknowledges the love already there from God. From this moment on we have agreed that our relationship to this child is permanently impressed by the good imprint: "in the Lord."

Here we have the theological basis for the protection of the child against excessive punishment by father or mother. Here we have by anticipation of life the theological basis for the protection of the unborn child against abortion. A child is not our property nor a part of our body: the child is a separate life whose worth is grounded not only in our love for our children but upon God's love. In his book *Reaching Out,* Henri Nouwen dares to state this fact in such bold terms as to maintain that from a theological perspective a child is really a guest in the home of the mother and father. He puts it this way: "Children are not properties to own and rule over, but gifts to cherish and care for. Our children are our most important guests" (p. 56).

In the biblical perspective, this is the theological context from which every human family derives its dignity; those who trust in this gift are able both to rejoice and to struggle with this intervention of the law and the gospel. But the worth of every human being is settled in the eyes of those who accept the law and gospel. The fact is that whether we know it or not, God has already loved us; it is the task of our life journey to discover it for ourselves.

10

Thy Neighbor as Thyself

You shall not kill.

—Exod. 20:13

The word translated "kill" in the Revised Standard Version is the Hebrew *rāsah*, which means "anti-social killing" (von Rad, p. 59), and is most accurately translated by the English word *murder*. The word is used forty-six times in the Old Testament, and, as Childs points out in his study, the largest number of usages carry the intent of the taking of life in the context of blood vengeance, in which the act of murder occurs because of hatred and malice.

The sixth commandment denies the right of any person among us to take into his or her own hands with a harmful intent the life of another person. We are commanded not to cross over another person's right to live. This brief mandate is greatly expanded in the code or "ordinances" (RSV) of the law within the books of Moses, and from that expansion the restraint takes shape in several directions. Within the expansion it becomes clear that because of this commandment individuals in the society are not allowed to take vengeance against those who have done harm; it is only the community that shall take action against wrongdoers. The right of capital punishment is a right preserved strictly for the community. The code also makes it clear that the community must exercise that right only after the verification of wrongdoing through hearings and by attestation of witnesses (Lev. 19:20, Exod. 21:22, Exod. 23:3). The community must make its judgments according to the provisions in the law and ordinances which become a safeguard against impetuous and informal punishment of wrongdoers. This commandment takes away from the individual the right either to initiate harm or to "even the score" when harm takes place. Both of these kinds of violence, murder and vengeance, are implied in the word *rāsah*. The law offers to us a four-word (in English) command against such violence.

The ordinances' expansion of the law also makes it clear that the commandment is not qualified as to the designation of those protected by the command. This, like all of the Torah, is a universal commandment, and the principle of equal justice under law becomes a basic ingredient in the ordinances. "You shall do no injustice in judgment; you shall not be partial to the poor or defer to the great, but in righteousness shall you judge your neighbor" (Lev. 19:15). This equality under the law is also affirmed for the foreigner. "When a stranger sojourns with you in your land, you shall not do him wrong. . . . For you were strangers in the land of Egypt" (Lev. 19:33, 34).

The restraint that is guaranteed in the principle of equal justice under law and equal justice for all sets apart the Jewish law from the codes of neighboring civilizations of the same period. An interesting contrast is seen in this provision of the Code of Hammurabi (Babylonian): "If a man strike a gentleman's daughter that she dies, his own daughter is to be put to death, if a poor man's, the slayer pays one half mina." In the law of the books of Moses, we each pay for our own crimes and the justice is prescribed equally.

In this context we can better appreciate the purpose of the technical nature of the code as it attempts to find proper equations, so that on the one hand the justice handed out by the community honors the harmed person by being equivalent to the loss, and on the other hand the punishments do not spiral in intensity beyond that principle of even exchange. One of the most famous verses of the Old Testament is a sentence from the ordinances that seeks to achieve this just and middle position: "If any harm follows, then you shall give life for life, eye for eye, tooth for tooth, hand for hand, foot for foot, burn for burn, wound for wound, stripe for stripe" (Exod. 21:23-25). This sentence is not so much a description of punishment as it is a limit upon the revenge that the community may demand.

Though the sixth commandment is stated in broad
negative terms, the intention of the law is positive. It
is a commandment in favor of life. Because human
life is so meaningful in the sight of God, we are not to
take life into our hands with a harmful intent. The
strong word *rāsah* makes it clear that this commandment is not correctly interpreted as a command
against the slaughter of animals for food. *Rāsah* is a
word that carried within it the intent of malice, the
kind of malice that is experienced within human
relationships and estrangement. But once the law
has made the protection of life from harm its focus,
we are drawn by the commandment to embrace the
law's positive implication. This deeper level is
expressed in Leviticus 19:17-18:

> You shall not hate your brother in your heart, but you
> shall reason with your neighbor, lest you bear sin
> because of him. You shall not take vengeance or bear
> any grudge against the sons of your own people, but
> you shall love your neighbor as yourself: I am the Lord.

We are not only to restrain ourselves from doing
harm. We are also to creatively do good toward our
neighbor. It is this latter direction that Jesus impresses
upon the Leviticus text with the parable of the good
Samaritan in Luke 10. The issue is not the method of
determining a correct definition of neighbor, but
rather the word *neighbor* is seen in the eyes of Jesus as
positive and dynamic: "Who proved neighbor to the
man who fell among the robbers?" The apostle Paul
also draws the sixth commandment out to this logical
conclusion in his Letter to the Romans:

> Owe no one anything except to love one another; for he
> who loves his neighbor has fulfilled the law. The
> commandments, "You shall not commit adultery, You
> shall not kill, You shall not steal, You shall not covet,"
> and any other commandment, are summed up in this
> sentence, "You shall love your neighbor as yourself."
> Love does no wrong to a neighbor; therefore love is the
> fulfilling of the law. (Rom. 13:8-10)

God's holy will in favor of life is the larger context
within which the sixth commandment states its
protection of life from the murderer. Therefore this
good side of the sixth commandment is the greater
mandate: How can I enrich and deepen the quality of
life around me, not only my own, but the life of my
neighbor? In the language of the gospel, the mandate
is even bolder. How can I bring new life to those who
have lost hope of life?

There are complex ethical questions that properly
relate to the sixth commandment, and we must now
try to put those issues into biblical perspective. They
concern the questions of suicide, abortion, euthanasia, capital punishment, and war.

We are denied by this commandment the right of
vengeance, which belongs to God alone. This means
that we as human beings do not have the authority or
the right to pronounce the last word on any human
being—others or ourselves. Suicide is an act of
violence by which a person arrogantly takes the right
of judgment into his or her own hands. It is
vengeance against the self. The reasons in each
separate instance are very often complicated, and in
many situations the ability to reason may be clouded

or totally confused because of despair or physical
illness. The sixth commandment offers no rules of
exception, and therefore suicide is against the will of
God in the perspective of the law, because it is the
murder of the self; it is the destruction of relationships. Suicide at an even deeper level is the distrust
of the faithfulness of God and his imprint of meaning
upon life, and therefore it is a violent act against all of
life. That is one of the reasons why this act has such a
devastating effect upon the members of the family
and the friends who are abandoned by this violence.

G. K. Chesterton put it this way: "Suicide . . . is
the refusal to take an interest in existence. . . . The
man who kills a man, kills a man. The man who kills
himself, kills all men. . . . The thief compliments the
things he steals, if not the owner of them. But the
suicide insults everything on earth by not stealing it"
(*Orthodoxy*, pp. 72-73).

Euthanasia, like suicide, seeks the solution to the
problems of life through death. The word *euthanasia*—
"good death"—promises that there can be *a good
death,* but the death we bring on to ourselves for any
reason is not a good death. Death is a foe, an enemy,
the spoiler of our stewardship and relationships on
earth. What we are promised in biblical faith is the
victory over death, not the embrace of death. Paul
quotes this deep longing of the prophets Isaiah and
Hosea in his affirmation of this theology.

For this perishable nature must put on the imperishable,
and this mortal nature must put on immortality. When
the perishable puts on the imperishable, and the mortal

puts on immortality, then shall come to pass the saying
that is written:
"Death is swallowed up in victory."
"O death, where is thy victory?
O death, where is thy sting?"
The sting of death is sin, and the power of sin is the
law. But thanks be to God, who gives us the victory
through our Lord Jesus Christ. (I Cor. 15:53-57)

Abortion which terminates an unwanted pregnancy is a violent act against a separate life. The
moral arrogance of abortion rests in the argument
that because a life is unwanted, it therefore ceases to
have worth or protection. But this argument is
repudiated in the law and the gospel. The orphan
and the widow are especially singled out for
protection in the Bible (Exod. 22:21-24), and in the
New Testament, because of the healing power of the
gospel, even the enemy is protected (Rom. 12:19-21).
Abortion treats the unborn child as our enemy. But
the unborn is not our enemy; rather, it is our life.
Because of the worth of each separate life, the
medical and personal decision concerning the possibility of abortion must be a very hard decision; it is
never a good decision, though it may be the right
decision among hard choices in that instance when
the life of the mother who is now present with us is
endangered by pregnancy. It then becomes the right
moral stewardship of life to choose the life of the
person who is with us in relationship over the life
that is only potentially with us.

Capital punishment is allowed to the community
in the law's expansion through the ordinances of

Exodus and Leviticus (for example, Exod. 22:12-17). The death penalty is prescribed as a punishment for grave wrongdoing to be executed only by the community. War in the same way is a community action determined by community policy. In both instances the community has made the determination that a person or nation or group are enemies that must be opposed.

The concept of just war has been broadly discussed and argued throughout the history of Old and New Testament theology. The issue is not simple; because of the reality of human sinfulness at the local community level, it is necessary that law enforcement officers are armed and prepared to take violent action against those who endanger the lives of other people. The problem of war is that same crisis, but it is extended to the international level. Martin Luther attempted to draw together the implications of the total biblical witness in order to develop a perspective on the issue.

> For what is just war but the punishment of evildoers and the maintenance of peace? . . . take my advice, dear Lords. Stay out of war unless you have to defend and protect yourselves and your office compels you to fight. . . . [Luther gives bold advice to his parishioners concerning the call to war that is unjust.] "Suppose my Lord were wrong in going to war." I reply: If you know for sure that he is wrong, then you should fear God rather than men . . . and you should neither fight nor serve, for you cannot have a good conscience before God. (*Writings*, pp. 438-70)

But the larger question of the determination of the community's correct stance toward an enemy has been permanently altered for the biblical Christian because of the way in which Jesus Christ fulfilled the commandments and covenants and yearnings of the Old Testament. Jesus Christ has taken the place of the sinner; this is the meaning of the cross. Therefore all of the punishments prescribed in the code converge toward and into this one man, who has "canceled the bond which stood against us with its legal demands; this he set aside, nailing it to the cross" (Col. 2:14). Because of this event we who trust in Jesus Christ as Savior-Lord must see other human beings in the perspective of their belovedness. They may not know of that belovedness but we who have ourselves discovered God's love do, and that makes all the difference to us.

This viewpoint deeply influences the practical question of how we must interpret the angry provisions of the code as well as the angry psalms in which the psalmist is praying for the destruction of his enemy. We know that Jesus Christ himself has taken the place of that enemy, and therefore those texts must be read in the light of their fulfillment. Jesus has identified himself with the sinner. That is good news for us because we are sinners. Now that good news is also an ethical challenge to us because there are sinners all around us. This redeeming identification of Jesus Christ creates both a positive and a restraining effect.

At this point in the consideration of the sixth commandment, we need to look closely at the restraining influence of this "holy interruption" of

both the commandment and the Lord of that
commandment. The restraining impact of our Lord's
identification with the enemy, the sinner, is dramatically portrayed to us by an incident recorded by
John's Gospel (John 8:1-11). Here the question of
capital punishment is plainly put to Jesus by a group
of Pharisees and Sadducees (see E. F. Palmer's
discussion in *The Intimate Gospel: Studies in John,*
pp. 83-87). In this incident Jesus places his own life
between the crowd and the accused woman caught
in the act of adultery. He slows down the total event
as he writes in the sand and makes himself the
central object of focus: "What do you say about her?"
The crowd shouts out to him, but Jesus turns the
question toward the accusers. "Let him who is
without sin among you be the first to throw a stone."

Jesus has done a remarkable thing. He has
restrained a crowd from doing more harm than they
have already done. According to John, they had
brought the accused person to Jesus not because of
concern for the preservation of marriage, but in order
to tempt him. This means that the crowd is already
guilty of tempting the Lord. But Jesus protects the
crowd from adding to that transgression the sin of
unjust vengeance. He has also refocused the event
both toward himself and toward ourselves. He
protects the crowd and the woman, but the shadow
of the cross is over this intervention.

A new refocusing is produced for us not only by
the incident of John 8 but also by the central incident
of all time, the cross and empty tomb. Because of this
refocusing, the Christian interpreter of the angry
texts of the Old Testament cannot see them apart

from their fulfillment. Jesus Christ has absorbed the anger of David's psalms of hate as much as he has fulfilled the greatness of David's psalms of hope. Because of the authority of the Redeemer we are therefore restrained, and because of the powerful love of the Redeemer we are able to offer a new strategy in the face of the ancient vicious cycle of the hatred between enemies.

The restraint element that is present in the law and deepened by the gospel of Jesus Christ makes me personally very uneasy about the practice of capital punishment by modern societies. The problem morally is that when a criminal has been caught and is then completely at our mercy, that criminal is no longer a threat to the community. Execution of the condemned has only the purpose of extreme and final public punishment. From a pastoral standpoint I am also concerned at the impact capital punishment has upon those who practice it. It harms the community because the community takes too much interest in it. We want to see evildoers punished, and that desire has a harmful and dehumanizing effect upon the people in the community.

It seems to me that the principal human equation that has been shattered by the violent criminal should be repaid by the criminal through a life sentence without parole possibility, in the case of murder, and that the criminal should spend those years in hard labor to repay the injured parties and the society. The lonely celebrity status of the isolated "death row" prisoners is not meaningful punishment. There are also implications of this that reach out toward the institution of prisons. Because life

is so precious, those who harm life cannot be
excused by human warehouselike imprisonment.
They need some spiritual-moral journey possibility
of which work and obligation to repay are essential
ingredients.

War is always a bad choice, though military confrontation is sometimes the lesser of bad choices. The
counsel of self-restraint which becomes the dominant dynamic thread of the sixth through the tenth
commandments is the needed ingredient in the
twentieth-century face-off between nations. It is the
first step toward reconciliation, and the slowdown of
that restraint provides time for the emergence of
greater positive realities. The spirit of the law is that
before we act precipitously, we should stop and listen
to God; we should learn and then act.

"Thou shalt not kill" is a good restraint. It is a law
in our favor that alerts us to the high value that God
places upon human life. It becomes one more sign of
how much we mean to the Lord of the law. Restraint
is one more mark of our worth that has its origins in
both the law and the gospel. Alexander Solzhenitsyn
argues for self-limitation between nations as an
essential first step toward world peace. "After
repentance, and once we renounce the use of force,
self-limitation comes into its own as the most natural
principle to live by. Repentance creates the atmosphere for self-limitation . . . the idea of self-
limitation in society is not a new one. We find it a
century ago in such thoroughgoing Christians as the
Russian old believers" (*From Under the Rubble*,
pp. 135-36).

11

Marriage

You shall not commit adultery.

—Exod. 20:14

As we begin our study of the second law in the second tablet of the law, it is important to note that the Deuteronomy text linguistically unites the second tablet of the law into a single fabric by repeating the word *neither*:

You shall not kill. Neither shall you commit adultery. Neither shall you steal. Neither shall you bear false witness against your neighbor. Neither shall you covet your neighbor's wife; and you shall not desire your neighbor's house, his field, or his manservant, or his maidservant, his ox, or his ass, or anything that is your neighbor's. (Deut. 5:17-21)

The effect of this unity in the Deuteronomy text is to draw together the seventh, eighth, ninth, and tenth commandments and place them within the larger framework of the sixth. This shows that the reverence for life which undergirds the sixth command is now carried forth into other interpersonal and social ethical directions. There is therefore a connection in the perspective of the Torah between the kind of disloyal hurtfulness involved in adultery or false witness and the destructive hurtfulness involved in the merciless vengeance of murder.

The word *adultery*, as it is used throughout the Bible, describes the unfaithfulness of married persons. "It is clear from the evidence that throughout the O.T. adultery was placed in a different category from fornication" (Childs, p. 422). This commandment at its deepest level has to do with marriage and its importance in God's sight. It is not a commandment about sexual sins in general, or about youthful morality, though there is an inevitable relationship between marriage and all interpersonal morality.

Two different kinds of sin are at work in sexual immorality in general, and adultery in particular. One is a hot sin, and the other is a cold sin. Fornication, sexual sin between the unmarried, is a hot sin and must be treated as such with all of the serious dangers that are involved in the carelessness and lack of concern for another human being that goes with this transgression. Fornication is warned against in Deuteronomy and in New Testament teaching as well (note Exod. 22:16-17, Deut. 22:28-29, I Cor. 7:36).

With the exception of rape, which is not fornication but, like murder, a violent act of brutality and malice, the hot sins of fornication from the biblical point of view are not as devastating as the sin of adultery. Adultery breaks a commitment that has been made between two people and destroys a relationship, the family. Far-reaching destructive results are the consequence of adultery in the lives of all those persons related to that family. C. S. Lewis is correct in my view, however, in describing most instances of adultery as cold sins. His nefarious senior devil Screwtape makes this observation.

Then there was the lukewarm casserole of adulterers. Could you find in it any trace of a fully inflamed, defiant, rebellious, insatiable lust? I couldn't. They all tasted to me like undersexed morons who had blundered or trickled into the wrong beds in automatic response to sexy advertisements, or to make themselves feel modern and emancipated, or . . . even because they had nothing else to do. (*The Screwtape Letters*, p. 155)

Adultery is the sin of abandonment, of loss of interest, of rejection, of self-pity. Most adultery is not at all like the highly charged carelessness of the young who have strong passions; instead, adultery is too often the desperate act of those who have gone stale in the afternoon of their lives and are feeling sorry for themselves because they are unhappy. They have no energy left to work hard on the adult relationship called marriage. Out of this exhaustion most people drift into adultery.

Dorothy L. Sayers has noted the same thing: "What commonly happens in periods of disillusionment . . . when philosophies are bankrupt and life appears without hope—men and women may turn to lust in sheer boredom and discontent, trying to find in it some stimulus" (*Christian Letters to a Post-Christian World,* p. 139).

The seventh commandment in strong and negative language warns against the error of adultery, but underneath this negative mandate, like a foundation stone, stands the positive affirmation concerning marriage. The point is this: the central concern of the law and the gospel is not the "negative" success of a man and wife who have never been unfaithful to each other, but rather the positive health of their life together.

Sometimes in a pastoral counseling situation a man or woman will say to me, "I have never been unfaithful to my spouse." This is one good and important building block, but it is not enough of a foundation to build a warm and nourishing home. The question I want to ask such a person is this: "But what have you done positively to grow in your faithfulness together?"

Marriage is the dynamic relationship of two adults founded upon the double foundation, first, of all God's faithful love and, second, the faithful love of two human beings. Both of these foundations must grow day by day through ups and downs into a living foundation for life together.

It is not enough to stand before God and humanity and say, "I have never murdered anyone." This negative achievement is commendable but hardly adequate to satisfy the intent of the law. Have you loved "your neighbor as yourself" (Lev. 19:18)? Have you "proved neighbor to the man who fell among the robbers" (Luke 10)? In the same way the family needs more than mere faithfulness to fulfill the mandate's intention, but it does need faithfulness!

The larger question has to do with the creative nourishment and growth of the privilege of life together called marriage. The law has provided a critical boundary line. But in this case, as with the other ethical commandments, it is a minimal standard. From it two people work toward the joy and the loving interpersonal relationship that make marriage what it must be in order to stand at its post of vital importance in the whole journey of human life.

Marriage thrives when the partners in the relationship have forgotten how to keep score at the minimal boundary lines of the law's requirement, because marriage for them is a maximum relationship. The intent of the commandment is positive faithfulness, which is the source of the most joyous and liberating possibilities in human relationship. Freedom between two human beings is then the exciting result of this positive commitment.

12

The Possibility of Communication

Neither shall you bear false witness against your neighbor.
—Deut. 5:20

The eighth, ninth, and tenth commandments describe single ingredients of the horizontal relationships that mark the human life of one person among other persons. These relationships are of private interpersonal consequence, but, now that the law has imprinted them in the tablets of the Torah, they take on even more importance. Let us focus upon the ninth commandment first of all.

The term *false witness* carries the meaning of untruth, the description of communication by deception. It is interesting to track through in the tradition of the ordinances the complex history of this social concern for truth-telling in the history of Israel.

Elaborate methods for establishing truth in vows and promises were developed.

An interesting example is found in the elaborate method of verification of the deed of sale of property that is recorded by the prophet Jeremiah when he bought his cousin's field at Anathoth. "I signed the deed, sealed it, got witnesses, and weighed the money on scales" (Jer. 32:10).

The concern in this commandment is the establishment of the importance of integrity. It is in terms of this basic issue that Jesus simplifies this commandment by his teaching in the Sermon on the Mount. "Let what you say be simply 'Yes' or 'No' " (Matt. 5:37).

The positive intent of this commandment is summed up by Paul as he puts forward the word *edify* into the discussion of the goal of verbal interpersonal communication. The minimal boundary is the prohibition against deception and untruth in interpersonal speech, but the intention is positive in this law as the whole of the Torah. The goal of human speech is integrity and edifying communication. This positive goal is a major emphasis in the Old Testament Wisdom Literature. Note the theme in the Proverbs: "For the LORD gives wisdom; from his mouth come knowledge and understanding; he stores up sound wisdom for the upright; he is a shield to those who walk in integrity, guarding the paths of justice" (Prov. 2:6-8).

The ninth commandment describes a human intellectual style and objective that has far-reaching consequences. More than the courtroom appearance of a witness is involved in the intention of this

commandment. The possibilities of social communication, business negotiation, and scientific advance-
ment are dependent upon the honest statement of
fact. Because of the importance of truth-telling in all
human society, fields of endeavor such as business,
science, and law have developed their own careful
methods of checks and balances to ensure the
reliability of facts, statistics, scientific discoveries,
and so on. This commandment therefore gives the
student of the law another example of the far-
reaching implications of the law. This ninth commandment in one way or another affects every
human endeavor that depends upon communication. It is the media commandment! It is the
commandment that concerns the scientist as much as
the artist, the financial negotiator as much as the
politician because it describes the thin and tenuous
thread by which all human beings are able to live
close to one another and understand one another. In
its most meager intention the commandment mandates the honest report over the dishonest report, but
at its fullest intention this commandment argues for
the greatness of language as the communication of
human fears and vision. It argues for the integrity of
the scientist and the artist. This larger definition is
whimsically defended by Oscar Hammerstein II from
the point of view of an artist-lyricist.

You never know when you will be found out if your
work is careless. A year or so ago, on the cover of the
New York *Herald Tribune* Sunday Magazine, I saw a
picture of the Statue of Liberty. It was a picture taken
from a helicopter and it showed the top of the statue's

head. I was amazed at the detail there. The sculptor had done a painstaking job with the lady's coiffure, and yet he must have been pretty sure that the only eyes that would ever see this detail would be the uncritical eyes of sea gulls. He could not have dreamt that any man would ever fly over this head and take a picture of it. He was artist enough, however, to finish off this part of the statue with as much care as he had devoted to her face and her arms and the torch and everything that people can see as they sail up the bay. He was right. When you are creating a work of art, or any other kind of work, finish the job off perfectly. You never know when a helicopter, or some other instrument not at the moment invented, may come along and find you out." (*Lyrics*, pp. 45-46)

Throughout the Bible there is great attention paid to the importance of the word of God and the word of man and woman. Faith in the Bible is understood as human trust in the word of God, which is the promise made by God. The integrity of the God who says what he means and means what he says is given as both a gift and a mandate to the human family by this commandment.

13

Interpersonal Morality

Neither shall you steal. . . .Neither shall you covet your neighbor's wife; and you shall not desire your neighbor's house, his field, or his manservant, or his maidservant, his ox, or his ass, or anything that is your neighbor's.

—Deut. 5:19, 21

The eighth and tenth commandments are paired by their similar objective. They both describe the relationship of a person and the accumulated relationships and property that go with the experience of living: the person and his or her spouse, houses, lands, and so on. The commandments recognize the privilege of the ownership of property. At the same time the commandments warn against inordinate desire for property. The word *covet* translates the Hebrew word *hanad*, which has at least two meanings: both to strongly desire and to seize for oneself (note its use in Josh. 7:21 and Mic. 2:2).

The connection between the human personality and the possession of houses and land is significant theologically in that it gives a double clue within the Torah that human beings are not regarded by God as disembodied spirits. Man and woman in the Bible are perceived in concrete terms and are never spiritualized. The human being is always seen in the Old and New Testaments as a real person in a real place who wears certain distinctive clothing, lives at a particular address, and has special relationships that go with concreteness. The names in the Bible emphasize this particularly: Simon son of John, Judas from Kerioth, James the short one, Thomas the twin. The view of persons of the eighth and tenth commandments is in the sharpest contrast possible to that of the late first-century Gnostics, who held a totally spiritualized vision of the ideal of man and woman. By contrast, the Judeo-Christian vision of persons is concrete and specific. Therefore the hope for the future contains this same concreteness at its core—not the absorption of the soul into cosmic immortality, but the resurrection of the body. It is the whole self that has meaning in the present, and the whole self is destined toward hope as well.

This concrete view of persons is imprinted into the Torah from its opening preface, which reminds Israel of the actual physical, political, and social rescue from Egypt. The concreteness is preserved throughout the mandates of the law, which in different ways make it clear that the law has to do with the real lives of real people here and now. From this standpoint we can understand why the biblical messianic expectation of the prophets and the psalmists demands a redeemer who shares with us in our real lives. A "phantom Christ" who is so spiritual that he is not fully human can never be the fulfillment of the Ten Commandments. He must be "born of woman, born under the law" (Gal. 4:4).

These two commandments affirm the concreteness of persons, but they also warn against the idolatry of concreteness. The greedy fascination with any part of the created order that causes a person to steal or covet is portrayed as a temptation to sin; it is against the will of God to seize possessions or relationships that belong to other people. We are instead mandated to respect a preserved distance between our own ambitions and the life space of other human beings around us. If the positive intention of these commandments is followed to its goal, the result in human personality is very healthy. It means that in our encounters with other people, we are to recognize their concreteness and their right to exist within a preserved space. Once we are set free from the temptation to steal or covet, we may then relate to other people for who they are and not for what they own. It is ironic that when we trust the intention of the eighth and tenth commandments toward the privilege of property both for our neighbor and ourselves, the effect of this obedience to the law is that the idolatrous importance of properties and possessions is diminished. Possessions, like the other concrete events of our lives, are a part of the larger whole that describes who I am in very much the same way that the clothing of a friend reminds me of that person. These commandments warn us not to tamper or interfere with such choices; they are protected by the law within the preserved life space of the human being. It is no accident that one of the common strategies of totalitarian religions or political systems is to eliminate that preserved space.

The Torah shows to us a more splendid view of man and woman. God is so sure of himself that he is not threatened by our individuality. In the same way, when we welcome the intention of the eighth and tenth commandments in our relationships to the giftedness we discover in other human beings, it becomes possible for us to welcome rather than envy that giftedness.

Part of the unique concreteness of human personhood is what may be described as the talents and skills that are a distinctive part of each person. These commandments set the stage for a stewardship view of life and community. When the neighbor is honored for his or her uniqueness and encouraged to express that giftedness within the total community, then the whole community benefits. But when envy and resentment become dominant in relationships so that the unique giftedness of each person is feared or repressed, then the community loses a profoundly important human asset.

The Ten Commandments conclude with this noble vision of the dignity of creation and of man and woman, the stewards of its immense possibilities.

14

The Greatness and the Crises of the Law

We must think of the Ten Commandments in three ways. Of first importance is the fact that the Torah is a statement of the will of God for all time. The law does not wear out, nor is it ever set aside. The psalmist of the law puts it this way.

> Thy testimonies are my heritage for ever;
> yea, they are the joy of my heart. (Ps. 119:111)

Our Lord Jesus Christ makes the same affirmation of the durability of the law in the Sermon on the Mount:

> Think not that I have come to abolish the law and the prophets; I have come not to abolish them but to fulfill them. For truly, I say to you, till heaven and earth pass away, not an iota, not a dot, will pass from the law until

all is accomplished. Whoever then relaxes one of the least of these commandments and teaches men so, shall be called least in the kingdom of heaven; but he who does them and teaches them shall be called great in the kingdom of heaven. For I tell you, unless your righteousness exceeds that of the scribes and Pharisees, you will never enter the kingdom of heaven. (Matt. 5:17-20)

The apostle Paul insists upon the same permanence of the Torah as God's spiritual law (Rom. 7:7-12). The law is the good rock thrown out in front of the journeyers that faithfully shows God's will for the journeyer and the journey.

The law is more immense than the pilgrim people of Israel to whom it was first given at Mount Sinai, both in original design and by implication. It is the Torah, the roadway, in the broadest sense, and for that reason the New Testament writers stubbornly refuse to nationalize its promises and mandates. Even within the text of the law itself, as we earlier observed, the international relevance of its provisions was affirmed by the references to the sojourners.

The Ten Commandments constitute a statement of the holy design and intention for humanity and the four relationships that make up our humanness: our relationship with God, ourselves, our neighbors, and the earth. But the law is also messianic in the way it points beyond itself. It is like the arc of a great circle; it is a part of that circle, but we discover its complete meaning only as the line of the arc is drawn around to its completion.

It is in this way that Jesus explains and interprets the law in the Sermon on the Mount: "You have heard it said . . . but I say unto you." He completes the arc toward its intended whole circle. The way in which Jesus relates his own person and ministry toward the fourth commandment has the same result. The parables of Jesus may be seen in the same light. In the parable of the good Samaritan (Luke 10), Jesus shows the full extent of the great design that is at the heart of the sixth commandment.

The law is also messianic in the way that it points to its author. As a great painting or literary work reveals the character of the artist, so the law points us toward its author. We discover the values and goals of God as they are expressed toward humanity in the law. John Calvin saw this positive role of the law: ". . . to keep them in suspense until his Advent; to inflame their desire, and confirm their expectation (*Institutes of the Christian Religion*, p. 300).

The law is messianic in a negative sense too. Bonhoeffer, in *Prisoner for God* (p. 79), put it this way:

It is only when one knows the ineffability of the Name of God that one can utter the name Jesus Christ. It is only when one loves life and the world so much that without them everything would be gone, that one can believe in the resurrection and a new world. It is only when one submits to the law that one can speak of grace and only when one sees the anger and wrath of God hanging like grim realities over the head of one's enemies that one can know something of what it means to love them and forgive them. I don't think it is Christian to want to get to the New Testament too soon and too directly. We have often talked about this before, and I am more than ever convinced that I am right. You cannot and must not speak the last word before you have spoken the next to the last.

The law identifies the awareness we have of our own need for God. It is as he endeavors to make this point that Paul tells the Christians at Rome that the law intensifies their crises: "Law came in, to increase the trespass" (Rom. 5:20). Just as a great plumb line is placed alongside the foundation stones of a bridge under construction, in a similar way the law reveals distortion or variation from the vertical. Once that revelation of the distortion is evident, the crisis for the bridge is intensified. We now know how extensive the problem is, whereas before we may have been ignorant of the real extent of the problem. The law provides a reality check which is good for us, but not easy for us. Paul compares the law to the truant officer who brings the youth to the Lord (Gal. 3:24).

This brings us to the problem of the law. It measures and to a certain extent motivates because of its inner truth, but the law cannot heal the brokenness that it discovers. We honor the law and we are grateful for its grand design, but we need more than the law of itself can give to us. The law brings us to the Redeemer, but the law is not the

Redeemer. The righteousness in the law's design must be fulfilled so that its goodness is realized and its judgments disarmed and resolved. The one who both resolves the condemnation of law offended and completes the glory of law fulfilled is Jesus Christ. This is the bold affirmation of the gospel of the law fulfilled in the life and death and victory of Jesus Christ.

We have come full circle to the author who speaks for himself.

A Study Guide

The Ten Commandments and New Testament Faith

Here are ten suggested studies for your reflection on the Old Testament law of Moses. They aim to help you understand the law of God both within its own setting in the Old Testament and also in the perspective of its New Testament fulfillment.

Study 1—*Exodus 19:1-6; 32. The Ten Commandments and the People.* Questions: (1) How do you explain the golden calf incident? (2) As you see it, what are the main causes of that incident? (3) Do you gain any insights into human beings from this event? (4) Are there twentieth-century examples of this kind of experience that come to your mind?

Study 2—*Exodus 19:7–20:3. Smoke on the Mountain.* Questions: (1) What do you learn about God from these verses? (2) How do you understand the hiddenness of God represented in chapter 19? (3) What is the good news in the first commandment? (4) How do you reconcile the portrayal of God's hiddenness with the personal pronouns of 20:1-2?

Study 3—*Exodus 20:4, Habakkuk 2:18-20. No Idols.* Questions: (1) What is an idol? (2) What are the weaknesses of idols? (3) Why do you feel that we are warned against idols? (4) What does the description of God as a "jealous" God mean to you? (5) How do you understand the three levels of the created order within this command?

Study 4—*Exodus 20:5, Isaiah 1:12-20. Search for Meaning.* Questions: (1) Why is the "name" of the Lord significant? (2) What do you think it means to "empty"—take in vain—the name of the Lord? (3) What do you feel is the cure for human vanity? (4) What is the positive opposite to the negative problem of emptiness?

Study 5—*Deuteronomy 5:12-15, Exodus 23:1-13. A Rhythmic Style of Life.* Questions: (1) On the basis of these texts, how would you describe the purposes of Sabbath observance? (2) Are you rhythmic in your own week? If not, what parts are out of balance? (3) As a personal in-depth project, design an outline of your own week and indicate the rhythmic sequences within it. Note the areas that need change. Make a contract with yourself for personal modification.

Study 6—*Exodus 20:12, Ephesians 6:1-4. Our Parents.* Questions: (1) When you hear the word *honor*, what comes to your mind? (2) In what ways does our honoring of parents move through transitions during our lifetime? (3) Why do you feel the interpersonal part of the law begins with our relationship with parents? (4) What is the ethical importance of the word *honor?*

Study 7—*Deuteronomy 5:17-21, Luke 10:25-37. Neighbors.* Questions: (1) Each of these laws is stated in negative terms: "Thou shalt not." How would you state each law in positive terms? (2) In what ways did Jesus intensify the focus of these laws in the Luke 10 parable? (3) What is the understanding of persons as taught in these commandments?

Study 8—*Psalms 1; 119:1-16. Way of Life.* Questions: (1) In what way is God's will as revealed in his law well suited to the roadway language of Psalms 1 and 119? (2) How is sin defined in these psalms? (3) Do these psalms make you feel uneasy? Why?

Study 9—*Matthew 5:1-20, Galatians 3:19-29. The Law Fulfilled.* Questions: (1) What does the word *fulfill* ("I have come to fulfill"—Matt. 5:17) mean to you? (2) Why does the law need to be fulfilled? (3) How do we fulfill the law today?

Study 10—*Jeremiah 31:31-34, Romans 3:19-26. The New Law.* Questions: (1) What is the crisis that the law of God poses for every human being? (2) How does the law point beyond itself? (3) In what ways do you think of the law as "messianic"? (4) What do you think Paul means by his statement that we are no longer under the law as our custodian (Gal. 3:25)?

Bibliography

Anderson, Bernhard W. *Understanding the Old Testament.* Englewood Cliffs, N.J.: Prentice-Hall, 1975.

Augustine. *Confessions.* New York: Modern Library, 1949.

Barth, Karl. *Dogmatics in Outline.* New York: Harper & Brothers, 1959.

Bonhoeffer, Dietrich. *The Cost of Discipleship.* London: SCM Press, 1958.

————. *Letters and Papers from Prison.* Revised and enlarged edition, edited by Eberhard Bethge. New York: Macmillan, 1972.

————. *Prisoner for God.* New York: Macmillan, 1954.

Brueggemann, Walter. *The Creative Word.* Philadelphia: Fortress Press, 1982.

Calvin, John. *Institutes of the Christian Religion.* Grand Rapids: Wm. B. Eerdmans Co., 1953.

Chesterton, Gilbert Keith. *Orthodoxy.* New York: Doubleday, Image Books, 1969.

Childs, Brevard. *The Book of Exodus: A Critical, Theological Commentary.* Philadelphia: The Westminster Press, 1974.

Davidman, Joy. *Smoke on the Mountain*. London: Hodder & Stoughton, 1955.

Driver, S. R. *Deuteronomy.* International Critical Commentary Series, reprint edition. Greenwood, S.C.: Attic Press, 1978. Reprint of 1902 edition.

Finegan, Jack. *Let My People Go*. New York: Harper & Row, 1963.

Hammerstein II, Oscar. *Lyrics*. New York: Simon & Schuster, 1949.

Lewis, Clive Staples. *The Screwtape Letters*. Bound with "Screwtape Proposes a Toast." New York: Macmillan, 1961.
————. *The Weight of Glory*. Grand Rapids: Wm. B. Eerdmans Co., 1949.

Luther, Martin. *Writings*. Philadelphia: Fortress Press, 1967.

Neher, Andre. *Moses and the Vocation of the Jewish People*. New York: Harper & Brothers, 1959.

Nouwen, Henri J. M. *Reaching Out: The Three Movements of Spiritual Life*. New York: Doubleday, 1975.

Palmer, Earl F. *The Intimate Gospel: Studies in John*. Waco, Tex.: Word Books, 1978.

Pascal, Blaise. *Pensées*. Translated by W. F. Trotter. Everyman edition. New York: E. P. Dutton, 1935.

Rowley, H. H. *From Moses to Qumran*. New York: Association Press, 1963.

Sayers, Dorothy L. *Christian Letters to a Post-Christian World*. Grand Rapids: Wm. B. Eerdmans Co., 1967.

Solzhenitsyn, Alexander. *From Under the Rubble*. Boston: Little, Brown & Co., 1974.

Tacitus. *The Complete Works of Tacitus*. New York: Modern Library, 1942.

Teilhard de Chardin, Pierre. *The Phenomenon of Man*. New York: Harper & Row, Second Torchbook Edition, 1965.

Von Rad, Gerhard. *Old Testament Theology*. 2 vols. New York: Harper & Row, 1962, 1965.